LIGHT
THE WAY
HOME

LIGHT
THE WAY
HOME

My Incredible Ride from
New Age to New Life

Frank Sontag

WITH MIKE YORKEY

Light the Way Home: My Incredible Ride from New Age to New Life

by Frank Sontag with Mike Yorkey

Print ISBN 978-1-63315-523-7

eBook Editions:
Adobe Digital Edition 978-1-63315-526-8 (.epub)
Kindle and MobiPocket Edition 978-1-63315-539-8 (.prc)

Printed by Friesens in Altona, Manitoba, Canada.

For bulk purchases of *Light the Way Home,* please contact Phil Van Horn at
(818) 517-5880 or by emailing BallPhild@gmail.com.

Interior design by Catherine Thompson (www.letitshine.us)

Cover photo by Kristi Chesley (www.kristichesleyphotography.com)

For information on Frank Sontag and *Light the Way Home,* please visit
www.franksontag.net.

DEDICATION

To those who've been told all paths lead to God . . .

AN IMPORTANT MESSAGE

A portion of the proceeds from the sale of *Light the Way Home* will be donated to two of Frank Sontag's favorite charities:

- **Crystal Peaks Youth Ranch** in Bend, Oregon (www.crystalpeaksyouthranch.org), which provides a ranch experience for children and families to learn about the saving hope of Jesus Christ.

- **Stella's Voice**, a ministry that fights sex trafficking (www.stellasvoice.org) in the Eastern European country of Moldova by offering a loving home for poverty-ridden girls.

CONTENTS

FOREWORD

BY

LEE STROBEL

author of *The Case for Christ*

Okay, I'll admit it—I'm an addict. I crave stories about how God redeems and revolutionizes the lives of wayward people. Stories like this one, about my friend Frank Sontag's circuitous—and sometimes miraculous—journey from New Age guru to devoted follower of Jesus.

Only God does stuff like this.

It's a tale of motorcycles and "coincidences," of spiritual confusion and a voice deep inside, of cheating death and embracing life, of alienation and reconciliation, of drugs, sex, and rock 'n' roll. But most of all, it's the story about a God who is very, very patient.

And persistent.

And gracious.

Maybe I resonate so much with Frank's story because I also was an unlikely candidate for conversion. In both cases, we started out running the other way from God. Maybe like you have. And in both instances, we met the irresistible Jesus. Maybe like you long to do, deep inside.

I didn't know Frank when he was a popular radio host in Los Angeles, chattering about reincarnation, astral projection, crystal healings, and channeling. But our lives were intertwined nevertheless. My experience with Jesus led to my book *The Case for Christ*, which God ended up using as a link in drawing Frank to Himself. Now we're bonded together as brothers in the Lord.

This is the kind of stuff that God does.

There's a good chance you will see yourself in Frank's story—maybe in his quest for acceptance by his childhood peers, in his fractured relationships, in his search for answers to the Big Questions, or in the way he was buffeted by the turbulence of life.

If that's the case, then wait until you get to the end. You'll find grace, hope, and a future.

That's the stuff of God.

A NOTE FROM FRANK SONTAG

What you are about to read is a story of my lifelong journey to find God and meaning in life. Even though I share intimate details about my past, I do not seek to glorify or excuse any poor choices I made. Instead, my intent is to shine a light on my life as an example of God's redeeming love. By the time you finish *Light the Way Home*, I want you to be inspired by my story of faith, hope, and recovery.

The stories you are about to read are rendered from my recollection as faithfully as I can remember them. Some names have been changed to respect the privacy of individuals mentioned within this book.

My great hope is that my story will inspire you to let God light the way home.

The true light, which enlightens everyone, was coming into the world. He was in the world, and the world was made through him, yet the world did not know him. He came to his own, and his own people did not receive him. But to all who did receive him, who believed in his name, he gave the right to become children of God.

—John 1:9-12 (ESV)

1

A TICKET TO RIDE

I've always wondered what my life would be like today if my car had started following that afternoon visit to the bank.

At the time, I was twenty-eight years old, single, and trying to chart a career path that made sense. Since high school graduation, I had tried my hand at various positions and trades, sometimes working odd jobs but always earning enough to pay the rent and keep gas in the car. I hadn't settled on what I wanted to do or who I really was, which was further complicated by a chaotic personal life exemplified by numerous short-term relationships. You could say I still hadn't found what I was looking for.

I guess what I knew best was the grocery business. I started in the supermarket industry as a box boy my senior year of high school and was eventually promoted to grocery manager in my early twenties. I didn't see myself working in supermarkets for the long haul, though—not after the evening when a punk pointed a gun at my head and coldly informed me that if I liked living, then I'd open the safe as quickly as I could. Looking down the barrel of a pointed gun had a way of crystallizing my focus as well as my memory.

So consider my state of mind on a spring day in 1984 when I was driving my four-door beater on the Foothill Freeway, otherwise known as Interstate 210 by Los Angeles drivers. Southern California had been my home since I was ten years old, so after twelve years of navigating Los Angeles' tangle of freeways, I felt secure behind the wheel, like a newborn wrapped in a blanket.

The 210 paralleled the San Gabriel Mountains, but offshore breezes blowing in from the Pacific trapped a hydrocarbon slurry known as smog against the sagebrush foothills, shrouding cities like Pasadena, Arcadia, Monrovia, and Glendora under a blanket of dirty air that obliterated the view of Mount Wilson during the spring and summer months.

I was used to the smog, which seemed to settle everywhere in the L.A. Basin and San Fernando Valley. What I was more concerned about was arriving at the Glendale Federal Savings Bank branch office in Glendora before closing time. You see, I was a "secret shopper," hired by an agency to go into banks, retail stores, and restaurants and report on my experiences.

Glendale Federal Savings was my last stop of the day. I had hit probably ten banks that day, earning $15 each time I approached a teller to conduct a routine transaction. My job was to determine if the teller greeted me in a friendly manner, used my name after I identified myself, offered me an opportunity to open a savings account or learn more about a car loan, and thanked me for coming by.

When I got back to my apartment in the San Fernando Valley suburb of Chatsworth, I would fill out separate reports for each bank I visited. I usually made $100 to $150 a day, which was good money back in 1984. As part-time jobs go, I liked the undercover work.

With medium-length brown hair atop a solid six-foot, three-inch build, I didn't look like the Little Old Lady from Pasadena—the stereotypical secret shopper—when I strode through the glass entryway of the Glendale Federal Savings Bank. I think that's why I was hired by the mom of one of the kids I used to coach on a high school basketball team a few years back. Some of her accounts were fast food chains like Kentucky Fried Chicken and Carl's Jr., which meant I ate for free while I graded the staff for their courteousness as well as the speed with which they delivered my order to my table or at the drive-thru window. For someone who didn't cook much, I loved the perk of free food.

I finished my transaction with the Glendale Savings teller and returned to my car in the parking lot. It was a well-used Chevy Caprice I had purchased from my sister's father-in-law. The car had been a piece of junk from the first day I took possession. As usual, the engine refused to turn over. Each turn of the ignition made it more apparent that I wasn't going anywhere anytime soon.

There was only one thing I could do—call the Automobile Club of Southern California, otherwise known as AAA. These days, I'd reach into my pants pocket and retrieve my iPhone, but back in 1984, cell phones weren't around. I thought about my options and decided that I'd walk back into Glendale Federal Savings and see how they responded to a stranded motorist. Perhaps I'd be awarded with an additional insight to share in my secret shopper report.

I made eye contact with an attractive blonde-haired woman in her mid-to-late thirties sitting behind a desk near the entryway. As I approached, she stood and straightened her navy blue business suit. Then she identified herself.

"I'm Heather Winfield, the branch manager. Can I be of some assistance to you?" she asked with a pleasant smile. (I'm using a pseudonym for her name.) Mentally, I added style points to my report for her friendly offer to help.

"Sure," I replied, appreciating her willingness-to-serve attitude. "My car won't start, so I was wondering if I could borrow your phone to call AAA."

"Be my guest."

Ms. Winfield waved an arm and urged me to sit down at her desk. I reached for my wallet and found my AAA card, which had an 800-number to call. When I got through to an Auto Club representative, I was told that it would be a couple of hours before a tow truck could reach me. Rush hour had spawned the usual rash of fender-benders and traffic back-ups, causing the delay, the voice on the phone said.

I hung up and turned to Ms. Winfield. "I guess I'm out of luck," I said. "They're saying it could be awhile before they can send a truck out."

We were minutes before closing time. Ms. Winfield looked at her watch, and then her face lit up. "That's no fun having to wait. What do you say we grab a bite to eat?"

I wasn't sure if I heard right. "No, you don't have to—"

"Really, it's no problem. I know a cute café down the street that has great food."

So we went out for an early dinner. She insisted on me calling her "Heather" and was very flirtatious from the get-go. Drinks were ordered, and as inhibitions were lowered, it was apparent that she was coming on to me. I wasn't complaining. She was trim, beautiful, and conversational. When the bill arrived, she grabbed it and insisted on paying. Mr. Bachelor didn't stop her.

"I'd like to see you again," she said as she counted out the cash to cover the food, bar bill, and tip.

She gave me her phone number at the bank, and I provided mine from my apartment in the San Fernando Valley. When we returned to the parking lot to check on my car, lo and behold, the clunker started up. I didn't need AAA after all.

At the time, I didn't think twice about why she hadn't shared her home phone number. I figured she was a career woman who spent most of her time at the bank, and that would be the best place to find her. Nor did I raise an eyebrow when she said the only time she could see me was on Sunday mornings and afternoons. I figured she was a working girl who didn't have much free time.

After the third date, we fell into a routine: we'd meet for brunch on Sunday mornings and then head over to my apartment for an "afternoon delight." Life was good, and my feelings toward Heather didn't change when she told me that she was married to a cop and was the mother of two children. I figured that was her business and not mine, so I didn't probe any deeper into her private life. That's how I rationalized having an affair with a married woman. I figured it was better for me—and for Heather—if we didn't pry into each other's lives.

A TRIP TO THE RACETRACK

We had been seeing each other for a couple of months when one Sunday, after *huevos rancheros* and a siesta, I suggested an outing to Hollywood Park. I remember the date: June 17, 1984.

"Why do you want to take me to a racetrack?" Heather asked.

"I've always loved horses—especially thoroughbreds. I just love the way these powerful, majestic animals gallop down the homestretch. There's also a horse I want to see run. His name is Lighthewayhome."

I had become fascinated with horses while growing up as a young boy in Cleveland, Ohio. There was something spellbinding about watching a chestnut colt, with nostrils flared and ears pricked, roaring toward the finish line with a jockey standing in the stirrups, shoulders hunched and surfing with the motion of the galloping steed. When I was eight years old, I had to stop whatever I was doing on Saturday afternoons at

5 p.m. and run home to watch the featured race televised from Thistle-down, a racetrack on the outskirts of Cleveland. My friends would lean against the screen door and implore me to come back out and play, but I wanted to watch the thoroughbreds run. This was appointment TV in those pre-DVR days.

I didn't ride horses growing up—that was beyond my parents' modest means—but back in second and third grade, I knew what I wanted to become when I was older: a racehorse jockey. I was small for my age, so the idea of riding on the back of a half-ton beast, ripping past a grandstand at 40 miles per hour with tens of thousands cheering me on to the finish line, stirred my imagination. Horse racing was truly thrilling—the "Sport of Kings."

For several years, I kept scrapbooks filled with news clippings about my favorite horses and the Triple Crown races. More than fifty years later, I can recite the win/place/show results for the 1963 Kentucky Derby: Chateaugay won by a length over Never Bend and favored Candy Spots.

My interest in horses never waned—not even after my sophomore year of high school when I hit my growth spurt and grew six inches from five feet, two inches to five feet, eight inches, thus ending my dreams of becoming a jockey. For a nine-month span in my early twenties, I was a professional handicapper who visited the racetrack every day—either at Santa Anita or Hollywood Park—and laid down bets. *The Racing Form* was my bible, and I studied the speed ratings and pedigree information religiously.

Heather was game for an afternoon outing to Hollywood Park—as well as getting there on the back of my Honda FT500 motorcycle. I suggested going on my bike because I had bought a motorcycle following the incident at Glendale Savings with my unreliable car. Since then, I had become a self-assured rider confident enough to venture on L.A.'s busy freeways. I stuck to the slow lanes—No. 3 and 4—and refused to "lane split," a practice where motorcyclists overtake slow or stopped vehicles by zipping past them between lanes. Lane splitting was popular—as well as legal—among Southland motorcycle riders, but I was too new to the pastime to give it a try. I had a lot of respect for the bike and what I should and shouldn't do on congested freeways.

THE VIRTUES OF RIDING
It was a friend of mine, Gary Stiles, who convinced me to buy a motorcycle. I knew Gary from Gelson's Market, a niche supermarket chain in

Southern California, where we both worked. He had purchased a Honda FT500 and loved it. One day, he zipped into Gelson's parking lot at the North Hollywood store aboard his sleek motorbike. I was impressed and told him so.

"Have you have ever ridden a motorcycle?" he asked.

I had to admit that I hadn't, which gave Gary an opening to sell me on the virtues of motorcycle riding in Southern California:

- half the cost of a decent automobile
- great gas mileage (around 50 miles per gallon)
- ease of finding a parking space (useful when hanging out at Venice Beach on the weekend)
- considerably lower insurance premiums
- and the freedom of riding under blue skies and California sunshine.

"You really should buy one," Gary said. When my friend added that he could get me a great deal at the same Honda dealership where he purchased his FT500, I gave this some serious thought. A few days later, I told Gary to get me a ride.

One afternoon, I carpooled to work knowing that Gary was planning to pick up my new bike at the dealership and ride it to Gelson's. The FT500, which is a hybrid street bike/dirt bike, was a 497cc motorcycle with a 32 horsepower engine and room for two riders. Gary, who rode a Monza red FT500, chose a black model.

I had a hard time concentrating at work that day because I was jacked-up to ride my new motorcycle home after my shift ended at 10 p.m. The only matter that gave me pause was that I had never ridden a motorcycle in my life, but Gary assured me that would be no problem. As promised, he was waiting in the parking lot after I clocked out. He patiently ran me through the basics: left hand for the clutch, right hand for the front brake; right hand grip for the throttle; left foot control for the shifter; and right foot control for the rear brake.

There seemed to be a lot to learn, and a half-hour tutorial flew by quickly. Then Gary wished me the best and turned me loose. He had picked me up a helmet, so I strapped it on and waved goodbye. I managed to get out of the parking lot in good shape, but at the first red light, I stalled the machine. I punched the electric start button and continued on my way. I loved the power at my fingertips, the rush of acceleration, and the feel and the sound of the wind whipping through my hair and screaming in my ears. There was also something exhilarating knowing that the only thing between me and the unforgiving pavement below was my driving skill and acumen.

Within a month, I mastered the FT500, which wasn't that hard since the two-wheeler wasn't that big of a bike. Feeling confident on L.A.'s busy streets, I drove my black Honda *everywhere*—except to the local DMV office. I knew I needed to get a motorcycle permit, but I rationalized my behavior by telling myself that I would get around to taking the test someday.

That Sunday afternoon, Heather had no reservations hopping on and wrapping her arms around my midsection. We didn't bother to wear helmets because motorcycle helmets weren't mandatory in California at the time. More importantly, though, I liked the outlaw image I projected with my longish hair blowing in the wind and a beautiful blonde on my back. To complete the look, I was dressed in faded jeans, white T-shirt, a thin black leather jacket, black boots, and leather gloves. I saw the world through black-framed sunglasses with polarized lenses that cut the glare.

The temperature was in the mid-80s on that June day, but as we left my Chatsworth apartment and headed south on the San Diego Freeway— the 405—the temperature dropped a good ten degrees as we neared the coast. Hollywood Park, built in 1938 and a favorite of Hollywood luminaries, was located three miles east of the Los Angeles International Airport and adjacent to the Forum, where the Lakers played. Hundreds of planes passed daily over the racetrack just before landing at LAX.

We were in no hurry to get to Hollywood Park that day. I told Heather that I was interested in watching only one race—the ninth and final race—because of a horse on the card named Lighthewayhome. I had tracked him on *Racing Form* and was intrigued by the closing speed of this six-year-old.

The parking lots were full that afternoon when we arrived just before the start of the sixth race. This was the 41st day of a 67-day meeting at Hollywood Park, and a Sunday horde of 50,000 spectators crowded the grandstand and Turf Club. Heather had never been to a racetrack before, so I showed her around and explained the betting system. Hollywood Park, like most racetracks, used a pari-mutuel betting arrangement where the odds were constantly changing in relation to the amount wagered on each horse. "But I'm not placing any bets today," I said. "We're just here to have fun."

We watched several races from the rail, and Heather's breath was taken away by the fury of the massive horses, running on ankles thin as broomsticks at near highway speeds. There's something about the roar of the crowd as the horses make the clubhouse turn and duel each other down the stretch, ears flicked back, hooves kicking dirt, racing neck and neck for the finish line. After one photo finish, Heather said, "I'm having a great time."

After the eighth race, I suggested working our way to the paddock area, where the saddled horses were assembling for the parade to the starting gate. "Let's take a closer look at Lighthewayhome," I said.

We saw him walk out from the stables, braying against a bridle made of leather straps that held the steel bit and reins in place. He was a gray horse, almost white, which was unusual in the thoroughbred racing game. I recognized the jockey perched on a small leather patch atop a numbered cloth: Laffit Pincay, the Panamanian rider who would become horse racing's all-time winningest jockey. The presence of an elite jock like Pincay told me that Lighthewayhome was a serious racehorse, worthy of my attention. He was one of the favorites at 3-1, but I was on a reconnaissance mission that day. Perhaps I'd lay down a big bet in a future race.

"Horses run in three styles," I explained to Heather. "There are front runners that prefer to lead, stalkers that settle in the pack before making a run, and closers that are content to run last and start driving the last part of the race."

"So what's Lighthewayhome?" Heather wondered.

"Lighthewayhome is a closer that will stereotypically fall 20 lengths behind the leaders. Watch—he'll be out in the ozone during the race. When he starts for home with a half-mile or a quarter-mile to go, he'll accelerate at a pace that's incredible to watch. It's crazy to watch closers come from way back."

The ninth race was a mile and a sixteenth with a purse of $28,000. We found seats in the grandstand and waited with great anticipation. Sure enough, Lighthewayhome looked like he was half-asleep coming out of the gate. By the first turn, he was eighth in a field of twelve horses, and then he fell way back. He was dead last in the backstretch.

"Watch him," I said to Heather. "When he hits the far turn, you'll see him make a move."

Not on this day. Lighthewayhome did not fire. He did not close any ground. In fact, he fell *further* behind as the main field sprinted toward the finish line. Rusty Canyon, a 6-1 long shot, took the win and paid $14 on a $2 bet. Lighthewayhome cantered home to an ignominious last place finish.

I was still enthralled by Lighthewayhome. Maybe he got dirt kicked in his face or had trouble breathing and lost interest. He was still a beautiful horse. I was grateful to go to the track with Heather and see him and the rest of these gorgeous animals.

Little did I know that this would be our last trip to the racetrack.

2

WILD HORSES

Heather and I filed quietly out of Hollywood Park as race fans headed for the exits.

The plan was to ride back to my apartment in the Valley—shorthand for the San Fernando Valley—so Heather could pick up her car and drive back to her family. As we walked to the parking lot, though, I felt a smattering of rain. Not much precipitation, but enough to dampen the streets. Motorcyclists hate rain for two reasons: roads become slippery when water mixes with oil and gas and raindrops feel like needles when they hit you in the face.

As we got on the bike, I turned to Heather. "Hold on tight. If it rains any harder, I'll pull off the freeway."

She nodded as we joined the busy post-race traffic on the 405 North. The light drizzle was intermittent, but I was riding cautiously. When we reached the top of the Sepulveda Pass, the Valley spread out before us in a beautiful tableau. The trace of rain had come from puffy clouds that passed across a powder blue sky. For this time of year, the "Valley of the Smokes" was unusually clear.

At the bottom of the Sepulveda Pass, I smoothly exited onto the Ventura Freeway, or the 101, heading west (although it's signed 101 North). The eight-lane freeway curves to the left, then begins a long straightaway when the interstate thoroughfare reaches the Balboa Boulevard exit. As we turned into the straightaway, the late-afternoon sun shone right into my eyes. It took me a couple of seconds to adjust to the sudden brightness.

I was in the No. 3 lane, cruising along at 60 mph. The speed limit in those days was 55 mph, a carryover from the gas crisis of 1974. In other words, I wasn't going that fast. Raindrops had fallen. While the pavement wasn't wet, I weighed whether it would be prudent to exit the freeway and drive on the slower surface streets to my apartment.

I decided to move over to the No. 4 far-right lane in case I decided at the last second to exit Balboa Boulevard. I flicked on my turn signal and looked in my right rear-view mirror. All good.

I was crossing the raised pavement markers and feeling the "Bott's dots" on my wheels when I glanced at my rear-view mirror again. What I saw sent my heart into my throat. A black sports car was absolutely *flying* in our direction. We were going to get hit!

Oh, my God. This is it.

The black sports car slammed into us at full force. I held on to the handlebars as we were catapulted forward. The bike flew through the air and came down on its side, but I still maintained my grip on the handlebars, afraid to let go. We slid on the pavement, sparks flying and metal screeching. Then I heard a distinct voice in my ear whisper, "*Duck*"—as in duck my head.

I had skied a little bit growing up. When my father took me to Boston Mills, a mom-and-pop ski area in central Ohio, he told me that when I was about to fall, I should relax and roll with it. Don't tense up.

That's what I did. Then I couldn't hang on to the bike any longer. When I involuntarily released my hands, I instinctively ducked and let my body roll on the freeway pavement. I don't know how many revolutions I made as time distorted and slowed down, but it had to be more than a few. I extended my arms and braced myself, tumbling like a gymnast performing the floor exercise.

When I finally rolled to a stop, I was facing *back* in the direction we got hit. Naturally, my body had gone into some type of shock from the traumatic event. I was in such a daze that I didn't know if I was all together anymore. Perhaps I had left a limb on the freeway.

Then I saw Heather, lying in the middle of the fourth lane, her head a bloody mess. The sight stunned me into action. I pulled myself up and started running toward her. Out of the corner of my eye, I saw cars skidding to a stop as traffic came to a standstill. A couple of drivers exited their vehicles and

rushed toward Heather and me.

I reached Heather first. She was crumpled on the ground, unconscious and moaning. I got down on my haunches. "We're going to get you help! Hang in there!" I cried out.

Heather didn't respond. A couple of people leaned in to assist her, and I rose to my feet, giving me a moment to assess my condition. I looked like someone had lit a match to me and burned off my clothes. My thin black leather jacket had practically melted off of me, and there were plate-sized holes in my jeans where my exposed skin had been rubbed raw. My gloves had been burned off my hands. What blood-stained clothes I still had hung on me like a phantom. I couldn't feel anything—not yet. The adrenaline coursing through my bloodstream was temporarily blocking pain messages to the brain.

Then I saw my motorcycle—or what was left of it—scrunched underneath the front wheel assembly of a . . . Corvette sports car!

I looked up to see the driver of the Corvette exiting the car and bearing down on me. The front of his shiny Corvette looked pretty messed up. "What the @#$% were you doing?" he screamed. "You @#$%! Look what you've done to my new car!" His red face was contorted in anger.

But wait a minute . . . he had mowed us down! And what about Heather, who lay bleeding in the road? And what about me? I was on my feet, but what were the extent of my injuries?

"You were driving too fast!" I yelled back. "What were you thinking?"

I thought we were going to resort to blows when I heard someone say, "Restrain the guy." Bystanders stepped forward and blocked his path.

Sirens pierced the air. I was surprised by how quickly paramedics arrived on the scene. They quickly loaded Heather into an ambulance transport. CHP officers kept traffic moving through two lanes, but the bottleneck caused a colossal backup that stretched as far as the eye could see.

RECEIVING CARE

I don't remember how I got to the hospital, which I later learned was the Encino-Tarzana Regional Hospital Medical Center off Tampa Avenue. I'm not sure why I wasn't directed to the emergency room for an ER doc to look at my injuries, but all I can recall is sitting in the waiting room, sitting tight until a surgeon in scrubs came out. "She's in bad shape," he said, "We have to do emergency brain surgery. Are you a relative?"

"No, I'm a friend," I replied.

"Well, we have to get clearance from a family member before we can proceed."

"I know she has a brother who is a police officer," I said.

That was a lie. In the heat of the moment, I didn't want the doctor to know that she was married—because questions would get asked. "I think I could find his number in her purse," I offered.

"Come with me," the doctor replied.

I was taken to the nurses' station, where Heather's handbag was being held for safekeeping. Heather had told me that if anything ever happened to her, I could find contact information in her handbag.

I searched through her bag and found Robert Winfield's phone number at home and at work. For some reason, I knew he was on duty that day, so I called him at the Newton division in downtown L.A. while the surgeon looked on.

"Robert, I don't think you know who I am, but I'm a friend of Heather's. She's been in a serious accident. She needs you. The doctors have to do brain surgery on her immediately, and it's not looking good. I'm going to hand you over to the doctor now."

The doctor took the phone and explained the situation. He listened for a bit, and then he gave directions to the hospital. After he hung up, he turned to me. "We're good to go, so thanks," he said.

I breathed a heavy sigh of relief. Then I asked if I could call my father. He lived in Burbank, ten miles away. It didn't take long for him and my stepmom to arrive. (My parents had separated and divorced when I was in high school.) The first thing my shocked father said when he stepped into the waiting room was, "Oh my God, what happened to you?"

I looked pretty banged up. I explained what transpired on the 101 as best I could, and then I told him that "my girlfriend" was undergoing emergency brain surgery. A fair amount of time passed as we sat there, which I attribute to the way time distorts under stress. After an hour or two, a nurse came out to the waiting area. She didn't have any news, but she took one look at me and said, "Has anyone looked at you?"

I shook my head.

"We have to do something about that," she said. The nurse escorted me to an examination room, where she and another nurse gingerly took off what was left my clothes. What I saw was pretty gross. I had bloody and cut-up limbs and enough skin rash to qualify me for the Tour de France. Some areas of my body—particularly my knees—were pitch black where the pavement had literally gotten under my skin.

I was told to stand in front of an X-ray machine, where pictures were taken of me from head to toe. Twenty minutes later, a doctor examined the results on a light box. He took his time reading the images, then turned to the lead nurse.

"These can't be right," he said.

"No, those are his X-rays."

Then the doctor turned his attention toward me. "What happened?" he asked.

I explained that I had been riding a motorcycle on the 101 when a black Corvette nailed me from out of nowhere.

"You're a very lucky man to be alive," he opined, which stunned me. At some level, I knew I had experienced a life-or-death moment on the freeway, but I hadn't heard a medical professional confirm that thought.

"You have no broken bones and no damage to your body other than scrapes and bruises. Were you wearing a helmet?"

"Nope."

"Interesting."

I was bandaged and treated for my wounds with ointments and salve. Then I put back on my torn clothes and returned to the waiting room, where Dad was patiently waiting. We sat down and waited to hear how Heather was doing. I figured it was touch-and-go in the operating bay.

My reverie was interrupted when Heather's husband, Robert, arrived. He didn't ask who I was or what I was doing there. Maybe he had gone down this road before—the one marked "Infidelity"—and preferred not to know why his wife had been involved in a motorcycle accident with a guy wrapped from head to toe in white gauze.

Instead, his first question was, "Where's my wife?"

"You'll have to ask at the nurses' station," I replied.

He thanked me and departed the waiting room. From a distance, Robert's patience and sweet demeanor with the attending staff struck me.

I didn't see him again, which was a relief.

CLEAN UP

Now that Robert had arrived, I could go. The nurses had given me a set of scouring pads soaked with iodine along with instructions to scrub my wounds. I was told that if I didn't get the black stuff out from under my skin, I'd get a nasty infection. Then I'd really be in trouble.

Dad drove me back to my apartment. By now, it was getting close to midnight. I turned on my shower. When the water was good and warm, I stepped inside. I scrubbed my aching body with the Brillo-like pads. The pain was excruciating. Pebbles, stones, and sandpaper-like pavement had either scraped my skin raw or were lodged in my epidermis.

Something else happened as I cleansed myself of road rash. The enormity of the near-death experience came down like a ton of emotional bricks, prompting tears to mix with the cascade of warm water running down my face. Everything about what happened on the 101 hit me at once.

I lay down in bed, but I couldn't sleep.

Too much pain.

Too much shock.

And then I remembered.

I dreamed this would happen.

3

ACROSS THE UNIVERSE

Three weeks prior to the accident, I was sitting at a stoplight astride my Honda FT500, minding my own business.

Then my subconscious mind heard a screeching collision of twisted metal, plastic, and glass—a circumstance so real that I involuntarily shuddered and started shaking like crazy. I looked around to see if any drivers had noticed. None had, but I still wondered, *What's going on? Is this weird or what?*

This wasn't a one-time occurrence. In fact, I probably had four or five more "incidents" leading up to June 17, 1984, each more intense. The last one happened around five days before that fateful Sunday. I was waiting at a stoplight at Canoga Avenue in the Valley when I experienced a particularly severe episode. I heard an explosion so real that when I got home, I called a buddy and told him what happened.

My friend listened but offered no insights. Thank goodness he didn't call the guys in the white suits and butterfly nets to spirit me away to the nearest mental hospital. I did feel liberated sharing these experiences with somebody else, though.

Then, when I took that late night shower hours after the Corvette ran us over, everything came flooding back into my consciousness. Once again I heard the sounds of the crash—the same eerie sounds I'd heard *before* the accident. The reverberation of crunching metal and broken glass plus the screeches from a motorbike being dragged along the pavement gave me the creeps. These sorts of "flashbacks" played on a continual loop in my consciousness.

Not only did reliving those moments freak me out, but mentally revisiting the crash scene made it harder for me to wrap my head around the reality of what happened on the 101. I don't know if that was the body's defense mechanism to shield me from the shock of the crash, but I experienced trouble latching on to the magnitude of what had occurred.

I was too banged up to work, of course. I didn't do much that first week other than stay inside my apartment and scrub my wounds. I was exceedingly thankful that Heather survived the emergency surgery and was given an excellent prognosis for recovery. After she was stabilized in ICU, she was transferred to Kaiser Permanente Hospital on Sunset Boulevard. Even so, I was racked with guilt for her involvement that day.

I remember my first visit four or five days after the accident. Before I stepped inside her room, a nurse pulled me aside and said Heather had been experiencing amnesia and didn't know certain people. "Don't be surprised if she doesn't recognize you," the nurse said.

When I walked into her semi-private room, I was shocked by her appearance. Her blonde hair was gone: doctors had shaved her head and wrapped her facial wounds and contusions in gauze. A pair of black eyes—she looked like she had lost a heavyweight boxing match—followed me into the room, but she recognized me.

"Hi, honey," she said as I took a seat close to her. "I miss you. I love you."

Oh, boy. I had come there to check up on her and show her I cared, but I also had another agenda: to tell her that I couldn't see her anymore.

Meeting Robert propelled me in this direction. The way Heather and I had been carrying on was wrong. I needed to walk the straight and narrow, especially because I had been given a second chance at life. This was a once-in-a-lifetime opportunity to start over—a reset.

Even though a nurse was in the room monitoring the visit, I didn't care who heard what I had to say. I scooted bedside and held her hand. "Heather, I can't see you anymore," I stated.

There was a long silence in the hospital room. "Why?" she asked.

"Because you're married."

"So? What's the matter with that?"

"It matters to me. You have kids. You have a wonderful husband. We both have a second chance at life here, and we should make the most of that opportunity."

There wasn't much more that either of us could say.

The next time I saw Heather was nearly a year later, when we were called to Los Angeles Superior Court to sign settlement papers with the insurance company that covered the Corvette's owner.

I would never see her again.

ROCKING MY WORLD

One week after the motorcycle accident, late on Sunday night, I was in my apartment, picking at my wounds and listening to KLOS, a progressive rock station heard on 95.5 FM. Whenever I was home I had KLOS cranked up in the background because I was a rock 'n' roll guy who liked listening to album-oriented rock music. I'm talking about tracks from the Stones, Led Zeppelin, the Doors, Jackson Browne, the Eagles, Fleetwood Mac, Bachman-Turner Overdrive, Foreigner, Aerosmith, and a new artist named Bruce Springsteen. KLOS's choice of music had a harder edge to it than bland pop songs played on rival KIIS-FM or KHJ, the Top 40 AM station. I wasn't into KRTH, or K-Earth 101.1, which carved out the moldy-oldie niche from the '50s and '60s.

Suddenly, at the stroke of midnight, the music stopped and a big, deep voice came out of stereo speakers. "This is Michael Benner, and welcome to *Impact*," intoned the host in a sonorous voice that resonated like a bass drum.

His command of the airwaves captivated me to keep listening. Benner said that for the next five hours, he wanted to dialogue with me, the listener, about a new approach to spirituality, the nature of the soul, and the development of consciousness. He declared that "ageless wisdom" is a consensus from all cultures about the spiritual reality of human souls incarnate.

Benner seemed to know his stuff. The wisdom of the ages, he continued, was metaphysical in its recognition of consciousness as the spiritual force behind all physical form. A spiritual path should lead to self-initiated realizations that were free of ego-based masters and dogmatic religious doctrine and be contemplative in its approach via feelings beyond thought, emotion, and physical sensation.

Whoa . . . Benner's self-assured observations fascinated me. I listened closely, and then Benner veered off in a running commentary that ended with a declaration that rocked my world:

"Motorcycle crashes can be transformational."

This dude on the radio was talking to me!

Ever since the late afternoon on the previous Sunday when the Corvette nailed me, I had been grasping for answers to *why* the accident happened and *why* I survived. Even though no one was killed, Heather and I *should* have been. The initial report from the CHP was that the driver had recently leased a brand-new 1984 C4 Corvette—the first fully redesigned Corvette in fifteen years. He was taking his shiny new 'Vette out for a Sunday afternoon joyride when he saw the 101 straightaway before the Balboa exit beckon like an open road in the middle of the Mojave desert. Spotting a gap in traffic, he punched the 5.7-liter small-block V8 and let her fly.

The Corvette driver never saw us on my motorbike for two reasons: one, he was blinded by the low sun in the western horizon; and two, he was speeding at 110 miles per hour, or 53 yards per second. That meant he covered the length of a football field (100 yards) in less than two seconds. No wonder we were sitting ducks. He never had time to react.

It boggles my mind today that a muscle car with a clamshell hood and a knifelike profile ran us over and yet I was able to walk away, albeit with nasty skin rash from head to toe. I'll be honest: back in the moment, I struggled with survivor's guilt. Why was I still alive when people perished in far more routine but no less tragic vehicular accidents? Why did I get a second chance at life?

Michael Benner sounded like he may have some answers, but like someone tossed overboard and struggling to keep from drowning, I was grabbing at the first life preserver tossed in my direction. When Benner expounded on multi-syllabic nouns like consciousness, realization, manifestation, and refinement, he really sounded like he knew what he was talking about. I was impressed.

Benner's five-hour show included taking calls from listeners sympathetic to his description of "ageless wisdom," as he called it. I thought about calling in and telling my story, but then Benner mentioned that he would be doing a lecture on Tuesday night at the Live and Learn Center on Ventura Boulevard in Sherman Oaks.

I could tell him my story in person. From what I was hearing, it sounded like the moon was in the Seventh House, and Jupiter was aligning with Mars.

SHAKING THINGS UP

I had another reason for wanting to see Michael Benner. I felt like some force was compelling me to leave Los Angeles so that I could get my head around what I thought was a life-altering event. I had some disability checks coming in—one of the perks of working in the grocery indus- try—and a bit of money on the side. If I kept my expenses low, I could go live in a mountain cabin somewhere, away from the hustle and bustle of the city. Then I could really find myself.

Michael Benner said that self-realization was the quest for freedom from worldly attachments and external coercions that exist in the culture around us. If I could get quiet and center myself, then I could become one in body, mind, and soul. When I freed myself from the trappings of the world, I could focus on preparing my mind and my emotions to recognize self-realization when it occurs.

To get started, though, I needed a mountain cabin somewhere. I'd have to work on that.

I drove my beater car to the Live and Learn Center and was one of the first to take a seat inside its small lecture hall. By the time Michael Benner took the podium, there were probably thirty to forty people from all walks of life in attendance. They were eager to figuratively sit at the feet of this heavyset impresario whose burly presence seemed to fill the room. A helmet of wavy brown hair and a trimmed Van Dyke beard lent him an air of authority. He looked around ten years older than me.

Benner spoke of growing up in St. Joseph, Michigan—across Lake Michigan from Chicago—and deciding to pursue a career in broadcast- ing while a student at Michigan State. He gravitated toward radio, which made sense to me. Benner had the pipes for the medium: a deep, boom- ing, and high-energy voice that sounded natural and relaxed.

He started in news and worked for the ABC-owned FM station in Detroit with the WRIF call letters. But his eye was on the big markets— New York and Los Angeles. When he decided to strike out on his own, he chose Los Angeles. No need to pack a snow shovel in the land of palm trees and a pleasant Mediterranean climate.

KLOS hired him in 1976 to read news but his big break came when he was asked to be a substitute host at sister station KABC—located across the hallway at the ABC studios on La Cienega Boulevard near the Sunset Strip. He filled in for Michael Jackson—the British-born erudite talk show host, not the pop singer—and did news breaks. In the late '70s, he got his own gig as the host of *Impact*, a talk show that ran on KLOS on Sunday nights from midnight to 5 a.m. You'd be surprised how many people are listening to the radio at that time of night, but that's L.A. for you.

When Benner was finished, I waited patiently to have a word with him. I told him that what he said on Sunday night—that motorcycle crashes were transformational—packed an emotional wallop for me because I had survived a terrific collision just one week earlier on the 101. I briefly recounted what happened in the No. 4 lane, and Benner listened closely. In response, he encouraged me to seek a path toward enlightenment. I replied that was exactly what I wanted to do. "I believe what happened on June 17 will transform my life," I said.

When I thanked Benner for his time, he nodded with a self-assured air, but I wasn't put off. He was the fount of all knowledge. He was the teacher; I was the student. Hearing Benner speak that night cemented in my mind that I had to get out of L.A. and try to figure out what happened.

In many ways, I felt like my journey toward something greater than myself started that evening.

4

YESTERDAY

His real name was Raffi Sulahian, but he changed his name to Morgan Christopher so that he could become one of the guys.

I befriended Morgan when we worked together at Ralph's supermarket after high school. For a dark-skinned handsome kid of Armenian extraction, choosing an atypical Valley name like "Morgan Christopher" sounded as far away from the Caucasus region of Eurasia as you could get.

Morgan dropped by my apartment during my recuperation. He had moved out of the Valley and was living in Lake Tahoe, where he had opened a pizza restaurant in King's Beach on the North Shore. He told me that he was renting a cabin in nearby Sunnyside, a village of 1,500 on the lakeshore.

From the excitement in his voice, I could tell that Morgan was having a good time in Tahoe and liked the slower lifestyle. Everyone in L.A. knew about Lake Tahoe, a large freshwater lake that straddled the California-Nevada border in Northern California. I'd been there a couple of times and knew how beautiful and pristine the area was, but it was a bit of a hike to get there: a seven-hour drive north of the Valley, more than 400 miles away.

Seeing Morgan got me thinking about how I wanted to take some time off from the L.A. scene and figure out what I wanted to do with the rest of my life. Maybe Tahoe would be the place to go.

I voiced those thoughts to Morgan, whose face lit up. "I've got an extra bedroom. Why don't you move up to Tahoe? Maybe the mountains and the lake will inspire you."

I was game. The idea of living in an unspoiled Alpine setting with a four-season climate sounded like a welcome change from the pavement-and-concrete culture of Southern California. I wouldn't even need a car, Morgan said. The cabin, located in a funky village along the western shoreline, was within walking distance of a market. I could get everywhere I wanted on foot.

I wanted to start over in Tahoe, so I spent the next couple of months selling most of my stuff—car, furniture, dishes, albums, and clothes—and putting in my notice at the apartment complex. In October, I was ready to go. Morgan was back in town to see his folks, so the plan was to hitchhike together to Sunnyside. It was all about saving money.

Our first ride got us to the high-desert city of Lancaster, about an hour northeast of San Fernando Valley. Standing on an on-ramp to State Route 14, with our thumbs out and holding a homemade sign that said, "Tahoe or Bust," no one wanted to pick up a pair of swarthy males in their late twenties toting big backpacks. I'm sure we looked like escaping prisoners. We abandoned our quest and took the Greyhound bus.

The three-bedroom cabin in Sunnyside was a rustic relic from the '50s, but the location was great—just 100 feet from the water. Morgan rented the other bedroom to a college-aged couple working for him in the pizza restaurant. I think my share of the rent was $300 for my bedroom. The musty cabin may not have been the most modern, but it was hard to argue with the view of the magnificent freshwater lake, which changed from shades of emerald green to azure blue during the day.

Once I got settled, I figured out a way to augment my only source of income—the disability checks. At one time, I had supported myself betting on horse races. As a confident professional gambler, I figured I could do the same at the blackjack tables inside the garish South Shore casinos just over the California border. Every Saturday night, my roommates—the college-aged couple—lent me their old truck so that I could sweep into South Shore. I was a disciplined gambler who gave myself a firm ground rule: once I won $100, I cashed in my chips. No more hands that night. No exceptions. Otherwise I'd lose all my winnings, slowly but surely, because the house always wins.

The $100 I raked in every Saturday night kept me in groceries. I

remember eating a lot of soup, though, and staying in my room reading.

What did I read?

Books on "spirituality" that I had picked up from the local library or a nearby bookstore, where used paperbacks went for 99 cents. I needed the insight of learned folks to figure life out because I certainly hadn't. Ever since that fateful Sunday, a handful of big questions refused to budge from my brain:

- Why did I survive?
- Why did Heather get hurt so badly when I escaped with a token scratch?
- What's life all about anyway?
- And finally, why am I here?

Heavy, deep questions to be sure, but after facing my mortality head-on, nothing else seemed to matter.

Here's another thing I was thinking: there had to be something else out there that made sense because the Roman Catholic faith my mother raised me with wasn't working.

BACK TO THE FUTURE

I was born on July 6, 1955, twenty-three years to the day after my father was born on July 6, 1932. No, I wasn't induced. That's just the way things happened on the day I arrived at Euclid Glenville Hospital in Euclid, Ohio, a Cleveland suburb.

I was christened Frank Michael Sontag III, completing a trilogy that began with my namesake grandfather. I'm three-quarters Italian heritage and a quarter German (from my mom's side), but on my dad's side, we're 100 percent Italian. What happened is that my great-grandfather got on a boat in Naples at the start of the 20th century. When he arrived at Ellis Island, immigration officials lopped off a couple of vowels and shortened his name from *Sontagada* to Sontag, which, interestingly, means Sunday in German.

Both my parents grew up in Cleveland. My father, Frank Sontag, Jr. was raised in an eastern suburb known as Collinwood. My mother, Jo Anne, grew up in Old Brooklyn, a West Side neighborhood. My father was the only child of Frank and Stella Sontag, who lived in a working-class neighborhood filled with Italian families in the 1950s. They used to say that all you needed was a strong back and an alarm clock to support a family in those days. Many worked in factories that stamped out auto parts or machinery equipment.

So how did my parents meet? Mom's cousins lived down the same street from my father's place. My mom, Jo Anne, often joined her older sister, Shirley, in spending time with their convivial cousins, who introduced Frank Sontag to them.

Frank, who was seventeen, first dated my mom's older sister, Shirley, but then he cast an eye toward Jo Anne, sixteen months younger. She was fifteen-and-a-half at the time but mature for her age. Her mother had been fighting cancer for years and was in and out of hospitals. Even though Jo Anne was the younger sister in the family, the responsibility of keeping the house going—cooking, laundry, and cleaning—fell on her shoulders.

Frank and Jo Anne's first date was to the Christmas prom. My mother was reluctant to go because of the age gap between them; she was a high school sophomore and my father was a senior. My father won her over, though. They continued to see each other while my grandmother fought valiantly against cancer. She lost the battle and died in 1950.

After my mother lost her mother, I would imagine that she was ready to get on with life. It was a different era in the early 1950s. When my father proposed during Mom's junior year of high school, she was ready to say yes. Mom was sixteen years old and Dad was eighteen when they got married in the Catholic Church in the spring of 1951. They moved into a rental home just a few blocks away from Frank's parents, who doted on their only child.

Much of my parents' social life revolved around dinners with Frank's parents. It was a given that we would spend every Sunday afternoon together, passing around heaping plates filled with ricotta-stuffed meatballs, pesto pasta with salty parmesan cheese, and thick-sliced tomatoes with *mozzarella di bufala*—buffalo mozzarella. Dessert was *cannoli*, a traditional Sicilian pastry, served with espresso so thick you could stand a spoon in it.

Frank and Jo Anne wanted to start a family, but Mom suffered a miscarriage. Then she became pregnant again, and my older sister Theresa was born in 1953. Another miscarriage cast doubt on whether Mom could have any more children, but my parents gave it another shot anyway. Knowing this back story, I know I'm lucky to be here.

I don't have many early childhood memories, but I'm told that I always wanted my way with things. For instance, Mom would give us a snack before bed, and then we did the bunny hop together to my bedroom on the second floor. Except when we got there, I wanted do the bunny hop one more time—starting in the kitchen again. This is fairly normal for toddlers, who'll do *anything* to delay bedtime. When Mom remained firm and said, "No, it's time for bed," coupled with a kiss, I'd repeat my demand to do the bunny hop again. This went on for quite a while, even after I turned on a steady stream of tears like a faucet.

When I took things too far, Mom was the disciplinarian. She never laid a hand on me, though, because she didn't believe in spanking. She'd take a toy away from me or make me stand in a corner for a certain length of time. I soon figured out that I couldn't budge Mom when I got a second or third *no*.

I don't remember my father ever disciplining me, however. Perhaps that's because I don't remember seeing a whole lot of my dad growing up. He was always working. I was proud of my pop because he was a lineman for Ohio Bell—one of those manly guys who shimmied up telephone poles and hung from the crossbars as he worked on connecting homes to the main trunk lines. Dad was always in the field, working long days and into the night whenever telephone wires went down during fierce storms that swept in off white-capped Lake Erie.

One of my earliest childhood memories is when my father coached a municipal football team. I was four years old at the time. The reason this memory is lodged in my mind is because my father received a "Muni Champs 1959" blue-and-red jacket after winning the city championships in Cleveland. He had a similar jacket made for me, which was a thoughtful gesture. I still have that jacket today, a souvenir from a time when a four-year-old looked up to his father with pride.

I looked up to Mom with love. She was the quintessential homemaker of the '50s and early '60s who made sure there was a plate of fresh chocolate chip cookies waiting for me when I got home from school. I think because she lost her mother at such a young age, she wanted to more or less make it up to her own children. Holidays were especially festive. Even on Valentine's Day and St. Patrick's Day, she would decorate the table and cook a special meal for the family.

The big holidays—Thanksgiving and Christmas—saw us at my grandparents' home. I was especially close to my grandfather, the original

Frank Sontag, who I remember as loving and warm. He was housebound because he was a diabetic who'd had his left leg amputated, so I'd go over to his house after school and play card games like pinochle with him. Other times, he'd sit in a rocking chair on their big porch and watch me play with other kids in the neighborhood. But his eyesight wasn't so good, which was another symptom that diabetes was winning the battle.

Papa and Nana, as I called them, used to take in Theresa and me a lot. Whenever my parents were going to be out very late, we were shuttled to their house to spend the night. I didn't like being away from home, but I wouldn't admit it. I remember one time—I was probably five years old—when I told Papa that Mommy and Daddy were crying for me and wanted me to come home, but I probably made up this story because I didn't want to spend the night at my grandparents. I preferred to be in my own cozy bed.

I looked much more forward to playing in the neighborhood with my friends. Coit Park was a great place to play on the swings or run and jump on the roundabout—a dizzying ride where we got the "whirlies." We swam at Shaw Pool during the summer and spent many a Saturday afternoon at Shaw-Hayden Theater, one of those old-school movie theaters that opened in 1919 with 1,200 seats. The Saturday matinee, a double feature, cost a quarter.

This all sounds like a typical childhood, and in many ways, I was like any other boy in the neighborhood. That changed, however, when Mom took me to the doctor one day after noticing that whenever I played outside in the cold, dry air of winter, I started to breathe quickly and shallowly through my mouth. An allergist diagnosed me with asthma.

After that, Mom was as protective as a mother hen, saying, "Be careful, honey," whenever I left the house to play with my friends. "Don't extend yourself."

"I feel pretty good, Mom," I'd reply.

"No, honey, you have to be real cautious."

Mom's nagging bugged me. I got sick and tired of hearing that I was a sick kid with no lung capacity.

My doctor prescribed an inhaler that I used to spritz a fixed dose of aerosolized medication into my mouth, where it was drawn into my lungs to open up my airways. I also had to submit to asthma shots twice a day, before breakfast and after dinner. Dad, who had learned to give insulin injections to Papa, would administer the painful shots, which terrified me.

When he wasn't around, I didn't get the shots. Mom couldn't have stuck me with a needle if her life depended on it.

When my asthma condition didn't improve, another physician put me on prednisone, an anti-inflammatory steroid that made me gain weight. I became a pudgy kid in grammar school, which didn't exactly fill me with a tremendous reservoir of self-esteem.

And then, in third grade, I received a boost of self-confidence from an unexpected source—the accordion.

The accordion?

Papa and Nana were actually the ones who encouraged me to play the ol' squeezebox. Maybe it was an Italian thing, but my grandparents thought I looked cute with the big box pinned against my chest, fingering the keys and generating melodies and moods. The accordion, Papa beamed, was one of the best solo instruments out there. It was like being in a one-man band, he said.

My mom signed me up for lessons with Frank Cardoni at Cardoni's Music, who taught me Italian classics like "O Sole Mio" and "Volare." I took to the accordion like Michelangelo took to paint and loved making music come alive through my fingers. My grandparents entered me in contests—yes, they actually had accordion competitions back in 1963— where I took home a third-place ribbon in the Ohio state tournament. The podium finish in an all-state competition took the sting off the black-and-blue marks on my chest from lugging the heavy instrument around the state.

Then my love affair with the accordion ended in a single night.

What happened is that I was among the 73 million Americans who watched the Beatles' historic debut appearance on the *Ed Sullivan Show* on Sunday, February 9, 1964. With their Edwardian suits and mop top haircuts, the excitement those four British pop musicians created can't be understated more than fifty years later.

I was eight years old at the time, the perfect age to be swallowed up by Beatlemania. I fell in love with John, Paul, George, and Ringo from the moment their emotive, guitar-driven number, "All My Loving," opened the *Ed Sullivan Show*. I bounced up and down on the couch, terribly excited by the screaming girls who threatened to drown out the music. The Beatles rocked my world.

"Mom, I want a guitar," I announced during the first commercial break.

Dad looked up from his newspaper, bemused by the shrieking girls but wondering what the fuss was about.

"No way," he said.

I shrugged my shoulders. Maybe I couldn't have a guitar, but that didn't mean I had to play the stupid accordion any longer. Talk about an uncool instrument. Electric guitars excited me, but no matter how much pleading I did in the weeks following the Beatles' appearance, my parents wouldn't budge, even as my accordion gathered dust in the closet.

If I couldn't have a guitar, I could at least listen to the Beatles. I had a blue-and-white portable record player in my bedroom as well as a generous $20 a month allowance from Papa and Nana, the equivalent of $150 today. (Yes, they did spoil their only grandson, but that was also how they showed love in a materialistic way.) This cash infusion supplied me with more than enough money to buy record albums and 45s. It wasn't long before I was wearing out the grooves in *Meet the Beatles* and other vinyl records in my growing collection. I added albums from other bands that were part of the "British invasion"—groups like the Dave Clark Five, Herman's Hermits, Gerry & the Pacemakers, and Peter and Gordon.

But I was sold out for the Beatles, my first love in music. I didn't even like their archrivals, the Rolling Stones. Back in those early days, you were either a Beatles fan or a Rolling Stones fan. You had to choose which side you were on, but nothing could lessen my devotion to the Beatles. My favorite after-school pastime was standing in front of the bathroom mirror and holding a hairbrush as my microphone while I sang along to "Love Me Do" and "I Want to Hold Your Hand."

One time after Dad saw me belting out a Beatles hit, he took pity on me and decided to get me a guitar. He tromped off to the garage, where he found a couple of two-by-fours lying around. Then he fashioned a faux wooden guitar with rubber bands as the strings.

For an eight-year-old whose imagination had been fired by the *Ed Sullivan Show*, I was thrilled to have my own guitar, even though it was more suitable as firewood than actually producing a musical note. I returned to my bathroom mirror to practice. Once I thought I was ready, I embarked on a mission to share Beatles music with everyone in the neighborhood. Stepping outside our front door, I imagined myself as John Lennon, the "smart one" and titular head of the Fab Four.

I'd knock on a neighbor's door, and this is what would transpire next:

Good afternoon, Mrs. Bianchi.

Well, hi, Frankie. What's that you got in your hand?
My guitar. I want to sing a song for you.
That's nice. What are you—
She loves you, yeah, yeah, yeah, she loves you, yeah, yeah, yeah . . .

I received a lot of smiles—no tips—but at least I was singing great songs while I played my make-believe Rickenbacker. (I read all the fan magazines, so I knew the make and model of John's guitar as well as other Beatle trivia.)

You see, music became my first reprieve from what was shaping up to be an awkward childhood.

5

CALIFORNIA DREAMIN'

Since my father was gone a great deal and wasn't interested in attending Mass, Mom took it upon herself to raise me "in the Church," as they say in the Catholic world. She made sure we were in the pews every Sunday morning at St. Joseph's Catholic Church, fulfilling our holy day of obligation. When I'd look up and gaze at the statue of Christ hanging on the Cross, the sight terrified me. Listening to Father McNally work himself up during the homily—his fair Irish skin turning red while his bulbous nose remained blue—was another indelible image I can't forget.

At home, Mom made sure we were "good Catholics." She required Theresa and me to kneel with her during Lent and pray the rosary, clicking off the beads with the rote recitation of "Our Fathers" and "Hail Marys." I found this to be a mind-numbing exercise in futility and didn't get it.

Both my parents wanted to be sure that we received a solid Catholic education growing up, so they enrolled my sister and me at St. Joseph's Elementary School, located on church grounds. I was taught by nuns who wore heavy black habits like they did in the *Sister Act* movie, but my second grade teacher, Sister Patrick Marie, could have played the lead role in a horror film.

She had it out for me. I don't know any other way to describe it. She must have not liked me because she'd throw erasers at me whenever she caught me daydreaming out the window. She had a good arm, I'll give her that.

Or, following some other act of malfeasance—like talking to one of the boys or cutting up in the back, she'd order me to leave my chair and come to the front of the classroom, where she would make a show of deciding which paddle to use on me. She had a choice, you know. There was one paddle hanging on the wall that was your typical wooden paddle. A second paddle, reserved for special occasions, had holes in it—for extra velocity.

Sister Patrick Marie then directed me to bend over, loosen my uniform pants, show her my butt, and not make a move while she delivered a wicked smack that stung like crazy. Maybe I got two licks depending on the infraction or her mood.

A spanking in front of all the other students! How humiliating!

These days, a teacher who whales on her students' naked butts would be hauled before a school board faster than you can say "parental lawsuit." But back in the early 1960s, parents accepted the authority of teachers and administrators, and no one batted an eye when antsy boys were regularly singled out for this form of punishment. (Funny, I never saw Sister Patrick Marie ask a girl to hike up her skirt and take one on the cheeks.)

I think Sister Patrick Marie had it out for me because I was bored by school and couldn't fake it. Things got a lot better in third grade when Miss Lange was my teacher. She was a beautiful blonde, warm and caring, affirmative and enthusiastic. I actually thought we were going to get married, but she informed the class that she would be tying the knot over the Easter break. I was invited to the wedding, which I attended. While I was happy for Miss Lange, I was heartbroken that we would never be together.

I have a picture taken with Miss Lange, not at her wedding but at my confirmation, wearing a red robe. Confirmation, one of the seven sacraments in the Catholic faith, is usually done when you're twelve or thirteen years old as a sign of mature Christian commitment to the Holy Faith, but in our diocese, they decided to perform the confirmation ceremony on eight-year-olds.

I discovered that confirmation was a big deal because everyone fussed that Bishop Edward Francis Hoban of Cleveland would be anointing the forehead of each candidate with holy chrism (a mixture of olive oil and balm) in the form of a cross. The priest teaching our confirmation class, on the day before the confirmation service, made a startling statement that really shook me up. He said, "You better hope you don't die tonight, because if you do, you have a black spot on your soul and you're going to hell."

What a restless night! I didn't sleep much, so I was very happy to get to church unscathed the following morning and stay away from the gates of Hades.

At the start of fourth grade, my life changed in a big way—and would generate repercussions that have lasted to this day. It all began with my new teacher. I don't remember his name, but he was a male lay teacher. Two weeks into the new school year, he met with my parents and delivered a bold recommendation: that I skip fourth grade and go directly into fifth grade.

I guess I was pretty smart. I didn't know it at the time, but I scored off the charts when I took the Iowa Basic Skills Test in third grade. My new fourth grade teacher told Mom and Dad that I was bored in class because I was unchallenged by the curriculum. For some reason, I knew all the answers and excelled particularly in math.

I'm sure my parents were flattered to hear that their son was so smart that he needed to skip a grade. The practice was fairly common in the early 1960s, unlike today. Mom and Dad said yes in a New York minute.

I actually fit the stereotype of the student who skipped a grade. If you glance at my school picture, you'd see a bright-looking, nerdy kid with slick brown hair and black horn-rimmed glasses—a typical junior accordion player. The only thing missing was white tape across the bridge of the glasses and a pocket protector full of pencils and pens. I was so nerdy that I even liked going to the dentist growing up.

What kind of kid feels that way? But my dentist had a fancy toy in the waiting room—an Etch A Sketch. I loved to lay the red tablet with a thick, flat gray screen in my lap and work the two knobs, drawing rectangular boxes and intricate designs that were like flights of fancy. One time, I had the following conversation with my mother:

"I want to go to the dentist."

"But you're not ready to go. You saw the dentist a few weeks ago."

"Can't I see the dentist?"

"No."

"Can't you call him on the phone? I'm sure he could see me."

I could cajole and plead with the best of them, but in this case, I really wanted to play with my dentist's Etch A Sketch. I liked using my mind to create something new and interesting. I always had to be doing something with my hands and my mind; too bad there wasn't a Rubik's Cube around back then. I also loved reading interesting books and acquiring new knowledge. I think I loved to read even more than I enjoyed playing with an Etch A Sketch.

In just a short time, my fourth grade teacher perceived that thirst for knowledge in me. They didn't have "gifted student" programs back in those days, especially in parochial schools, so if a child was precocious in the classroom, then teachers and administrators believed that accelerating the grade level was the best route to go.

The reality, however, was that they plucked a nine-year-old comfortable with his surroundings and suddenly thrust him into a new classroom setting with ten- and eleven-year-olds. This was a disaster in the making for an asthmatic kid whose mom repeatedly reminded him he was a sickly kid and shouldn't exert himself.

CHANGES AHEAD

Mom was having her share of health issues as well. While I was being accelerated at St. Joe's, she came down with pneumonia, which triggered problems with her eyes and ears. The symptoms were so serious that she sought treatment at the famed Cleveland Clinic, where she was diagnosed with Ménière's disease, a disorder of the inner ear that affects your hearing and balance.

Mom had an aunt living in Los Angeles, and when she heard that Mom was suffering attacks from Ménière's disease that lasted anywhere from several hours to several days, she wrote and suggested that she see Dr. William House, who had a clinic on 3rd and Alvarado in downtown L.A.

Dr. House had been having success treating those with inner ear problems, so Mom and Dad flew out to L.A. for a couple of weeks to see if that was true while Theresa and I stayed with Papa and Nana.

The year was 1964, sometime during spring. Dad came home raving about the seventy-degree weather and swaying palm trees under an eggshell-blue sky. Working outdoors and hanging from a telephone pole in frigid temperatures lost a lot of its allure after that trip. My dad couldn't stop talking about how great Los Angeles was.

I think my grandparents saw which way the wind was blowing and didn't want to lose their only child to a California wanderlust. They bought my parents a house in Eastlake, which was a curious decision because that placed our family a good eight to ten miles away from my grandparents instead of a quarter-mile distance. The move also meant I was starting the fifth grade—as a student who skipped—in a new school named St. Justin Martyr. I would be stepping into a classroom where I knew no one and had no friends.

I was thrown for an emotional loop. I could tell that kids were talking about me, so I did the *opposite* of what a smart student should do—I played dumb. I didn't raise my hand in class, even when I knew the answer long before the others. I purposely didn't finish tests so I wouldn't get the best grade. I kept my head down and worked hard at doing the minimum.

My strategy was working when I got thrown another curveball: my parents decided to move the family to Los Angeles during the fall of 1964. They had all sorts of good reasons for picking up stakes and moving out West:

- Mom's treatment with Dr. House had gone better than expected, so she wanted to continue to see him.
- My asthma symptoms would be helped tremendously by getting out of the cold.
- I had developed allergy problems when we moved to Eastlake because our home was surrounded by vacant land filled with weeds and pollen, so a move west would take care of that problem.
- Mom had lots of family in L.A., so we'd have plenty of support from the Zahler aunts and uncles.
- Dad had an electrician's job at a Hollywood film studio lined up, thanks to a recommendation from a neighbor of one of Mom's aunts.

Since I wasn't happy at St. Justin Martyr, I was eager to try something else. I had never been west of the Ohio border, but from the perspective of a nine-year-old kid growing up in a Rust Belt city, Southern California sounded like Shangri-la.

THE TRIP WEST

My dad moved out to California first so that Theresa and I could finish the first semester in Eastlake. Dad lived with my mom's aunt and uncle, Rose and Sam, and worked for Universal Studios on the night crew that rigged and hung lights for the next day's shoot. You better believe it that all my classmates in Ohio knew that my pop worked in Hollywood.

When school was out, my mom, sister, and I flew out west and moved in with Aunt Rose and Uncle Sam. After settling in, my parents found an apartment on Coldwater Canyon Boulevard in Van Nuys. We were there until their Eastlake home found a buyer. Once that happened, my parents purchased a three-bedroom, two-story home with generous square footage for the time—around 2,300 square feet—off of Chandler Boulevard in Van Nuys. The address was 5420 Ethel Avenue, and I still remember our phone number: (213) 988-5088. With aunts, uncles, and cousins nearby, we felt like we were looked after.

Mom really wanted Theresa and me to be in a parochial school, but the money wasn't there, so we attended Robert A. Millikan Middle School—named after a Nobel Prize winner for physics. Public school was quite a cultural shock. Kids got up and left the classroom whenever they wanted to. They talked loudly to their neighbors, even when the teacher was diagramming a math problem or verb conjugation on the blackboard. Students had way more freedom than what I was used to seeing in the classroom. I know Sister Patrick Marie would've straightened out those kids in a hurry with a few well-thrown erasers.

Mom promised Theresa and me that we could go to a Catholic high school, and she made good on her word. Theresa went to the all-girls Providence High in Burbank, and I enrolled at Notre Dame High School in Sherman Oaks—all boys and all testosterone.

Keep in mind that I had skipped, so I was a year behind in puberty and physical maturation. Taking a shower after P.E. class my freshman year was humiliating. The jibes from hairy seniors are seared in my memory. Being called "bald eagle" in the showers was bad enough, but then someone cleverly figured out that my last name of Sontag could be changed to "son of a fag." Half the school thought that was the funniest thing they ever heard. I can still hear that taunt today.

That was even more reason to keep my head down and play dumb in the classroom. No reason to call any more attention to myself. I didn't answer questions in class and picked the wrong answers on multiple-choice tests. I got very average grades. Lots of Cs, the occasional B, and the rare A when I was engaged in the subject matter.

As bad as school was, life was worse at home because there were times when Dad disappeared—for days. We had no idea where he was. Sure, working on Hollywood sets as a gaffer—a chief electrician— demanded long hours, but he had to stay *somewhere* after the day's shooting was done. When he'd finally come home following a five-day sojourn, Mom would demand to know where he'd been.

"@#$% you!" was a typical response, which would set off fireworks. When the yelling and screaming reached fever-pitch levels, I hid in my bedroom until the coast was clear.

Things would calm down some, but Theresa and I felt like we were walking on proverbial eggshells around the house. I never knew when Dad would blow a fuse, but I knew it could be any moment since he was in a bad mood all the time.

One Saturday afternoon, I was minding my own business, watching TV from the living room couch. Maybe Dad thought I should be outside doing something more useful with my time, or maybe he was still smarting from his last argument with Mom. Whatever the reason, I bothered him when I was watching TV. When he walked over to me and I saw the livid look on his face, I knew I was in trouble. I braced myself for the blows, but he still managed to find an opening and slap me in the face.

"Go to your room!" he screamed.

The left side of my face stung from the blow, but my pride took a greater hit. I skittered to my bedroom and put the Doors' debut album on my turntable. A powerful, dark song took up most of Side 2: "The End," a nearly twelve-minute ode to a guy who wanted to shoot his father.

I didn't want to kill my father. I wasn't capable of that. I loved him. But I wanted to end my mother's pain. Many nights when my father was away and we had no idea where he was, my mother kneeled before a picture of Mary, the mother of God, and prayed her rosary between sobs. She was a martyr Catholic wife and mom, abandoned by her husband. A doormat.

While my heart broke to see Mom in this weak and painful condition, watching nothing happen in response to her prayers left me with a bad taste about faith. If God ignored the prayers of a weeping woman wronged in life and in marriage, why would He ever listen to me?

It was right around this volatile time that I stopped going to Mass at

St. Francis de Sales in Sherman Oaks. Mom didn't have it in her to rally the troops and make us go on Sunday mornings. I had lost any flagging desire to go to Mass anyway.

I was still attending a Catholic high school, but similar to how I put forth the minimum effort in the classroom, I decided to give lip service to religion.

6

AQUARIUS/LET THE
SUN SHINE IN

In the summer of 1969, I turned fourteen years old. There were a lot of things happening that tumultuous summer, starting with Apollo 11 astronauts Neil Armstrong and Buzz Aldrin landing on the moon, followed by the Tate-LaBianca murders. In early August, actress Sharon Tate, wife of film director Roman Polanski, was savagely stabbed to death, along with four others, in Benedict Canyon, an exclusive enclave just three miles away from Van Nuys as the crow flies. I remember the palpable fear that swept over the Valley.

The soundtrack for the summer was a 5th Dimension medley of two songs written for the musical *Hair*, "Aquarius/Let the Sun Shine In," but there was no sun shining in our household. My parents were still fighting. Whenever there was a major blow-up, which was often, Dad used that as a convenient excuse to haul off.

We wouldn't see him for a week, sometimes two. Then he'd return out of the blue, as if nothing out of the ordinary had happened. The three of us were expected to pretend that nothing was amiss. You could count the days, sometimes hours, though, before Mom and Dad would pick up their last argument from where they had left off. Their tension-filled exchange would invariably escalate into a war of words, and then Dad would slam the front door as he took off again. We could count on not seeing him for a while.

I always knew when Dad was leaving—or coming back. He drove a '65 El Camino, a coupe utility vehicle where the front half looked like a Chevy Chevelle sedan, but the back half was like a flatbed truck. He modified his white El Camino with glasspacks—a type of muffler that gave his car a throaty engine note.

One summer evening in 1969, I heard Dad's thundering El Camino roll into the driveway. He'd been gone a week, but I didn't care that he'd come back. I had so much anger built up in me.

He didn't come into the house, which wasn't like him. Instead, I heard him banging around in the garage. I went to the living room window to check out what was going on. I saw him on a stepladder attaching a basketball backboard and rim to the garage.

I stepped through the front door and approached. "Welcome, home," I said in the most sarcastic voice I could muster.

Dad grunted and continued working a wrench from his perch.

"What are you doing?" I asked.

"This is for you. A basketball hoop."

I could see that. "Fine," I said. "I just want you to know that I will never, ever, ever use that."

Having gotten that off my chest, I turned on my heels and stormed back into the house.

Why would I play basketball? I had never dribbled a ball in my life. Never even taken a shot at a basket rim. I was a sickly kid, remember? I only tried out for youth sports teams twice. The first happened at eight years old when Dad signed me up to play in a Pop Warner football league, but I had to quit midway through the season because of my asthma problems. After we moved to Los Angeles, Dad convinced me to go out for Little League baseball. At the tryouts, the coaches had everyone run the bases. The fastest time was twelve seconds. I huffed and puffed and gave it everything I had. As I rounded third and headed for home, I was wheezing like crazy, but I finished in thirteen seconds, an excellent time.

Dad patted me on the back. "I'm really proud of you, son," he said. Hearing him say that filled my sails. In Little League, you play according to your age, not your grade, so I was competing against my peers. Despite my small height, I ended up being a good little baseball player and made the All-Star team.

But let's face it: baseball is not a strenuous game, especially when you play first base like I did. After a few years of living in Los Angeles, it was evident that I hadn't gotten over my asthma problems as we'd hoped. Consequently, Mom was all over me, fussing about my health, practically smothering me with attention. She gave me no room to breathe.

A few months earlier, she escorted to me a specialist, who ordered lab work. Blood was drawn, a urine cup was filled.

When we returned to find out the results, I was startled by the look on the doctor's face when he walked into the examination room. Mom leaned forward in her chair, clutching her purse.

The doctor grimaced. "I have some bad news," he announced.

I waited for the other shoe to drop.

"You have hypoglycemia," he intoned, a look of concern written on his face.

I had no idea what this six-syllable word meant, but if a medical doctor in a white lab coat said I had hypoglycemia, then it must be really bad—worse than cancer.

On cue, my mother broke down and cried. "This is horrible news," she said, dabbing at tears. "What are we going to do?"

The doctor looked up from his chart and met my eyes. "You'll never be active," he declared. "You'll have to be careful when you're walking outside, especially in the wind, because you have no lung capacity."

Whoa . . . this sounded like I could die from riding a bike.

I trudged back to the car, devastated by the news.

When I asked Mom what hypoglycemia was, she said it was a sign of abnormally low levels of blood sugar, or glucose, which is the body's main energy source. Having hypoglycemia meant that I'd always feel weak and suffer headaches from low blood sugar.

I guess I wasn't going to die, but it didn't sound like I was going to have a very fun life. No wonder I was always the last boy picked in the schoolyard and the first boy picked on in the hallways. I was a year younger than my classmates, and with a July birthday, a year behind even the youngest person in my class. The runt of the litter.

When we got home, I didn't know what else to do other than throw myself onto my bed and cry into my pillow. You could say I threw a major pity party.

And then I had an epiphany of sorts. If I was going have such a crummy life, I might as well go down fighting. I recall lying on my bed and thinking, *You know what? I'm not buying this.*

I pulled myself to my feet and put on some shorts and sneakers. Then I found Mom in the living room.

"What are you doing?" she asked. I didn't wear shorts that much. My uniform was blue jeans and T-shirts.

"I'm going to start running."

"Honey, you can't. Didn't you hear the doctor? You can't do anything active."

"I don't care."

I turned out of the driveway and took a right onto Ethel Avenue, a pleasant, tree-lined street. I didn't start jogging. I wasn't in shape to do that. But I could walk, and that's what I did for the next half hour or so. I held the inhaler in my hand like it was a life preserver, but I was determined that I was going to push it one way or another.

The next day, I walked further. The next day, I lasted for an hour strolling through the neighborhood. The day after that, I lifted my feet and jogged a bit. When I tired, I walked. By week's end, I was running lightly. Instead of making me feel weaker, the exercise gave me a lift. I felt like I was building stamina.

One warm summer evening, feeling good about my wind, I flipped on a light that illuminated our driveway. Dad had left the roost again, but I noticed he had purchased a basketball and left it in the garage. I picked up the leather ball and looked at it. I spun it in my hands and got used to the weight of the ball. I bounced it a few times and slowly dribbled my way to about fifteen feet away from the basketball rim. Free-throw distance.

Like I said, I had never shot a basketball in my life. I bounced the ball once and then brought it up to my hands. I flicked my wrists and watched the ball spin toward the basketball standard. My shot swished through the orange rim.

I still remember the sweet sound of nothing but net. I was hooked on basketball immediately.

From that evening forward, I spent hours on end in the driveway, making lay-ups and shooting jump shots. Hours and hours. I rustled up guys in the neighborhood for three-on-three half-court contests. On Saturday mornings, my buddies and I would start playing games to ten baskets and stay out there all day, losers sitting out. When Mom announced that dinner was ready, eating didn't appeal to me. I wanted to continue playing hoops, especially if my teammates and I were on a winning streak.

The girls next door noticed that I was spending all my free time practicing jump shots and competing in pick-up games. I say girls, plural, because there were five of them. Let's call them the Johnsons. They were a good Catholic family because they named all five girls after Mary, the mother of Jesus. Their birth order was Mary Catherine, Mary Anne, Mary Ellen, Mary Louise, and Mary Christine.

One night, I was shooting hoops in the driveway when I looked over and saw three sets of eyes watching me. A trio of girls stood behind a five-foot cinder block wall separating our driveway from the Johnsons.

Having three cuties watching me shoot around made me feel good. I showed them a couple of moves, swished a few jump shots, and then moseyed over to the wall to chat them up. One was older than me, one was the same age, and one was a year younger—Mary Christine. She was a gorgeous blonde, the eye candy you'd expect to see at a Southern California beach. Her blonde hair was streaked from the sun, and her bronze skin spoke of vitality and youth. She was also thirteen years old.

Mary Christine took my breath away. I fell in love on the spot. She saw something in me as well because she started coming over every night—around 10 o'clock or so—to talk with me. Our house was built in such a way that my bedroom adjoined their property but no wall or fence separated our homes. Mary Christine would sneak out—she had a domineering dad and had to be careful—and stand on the meter box next to my bedroom window. We spoke sweet-nothings to each other, flirted like the embarrassed adolescents that we were, and then we started meeting behind the house for make-out sessions. She was the first girl I ever kissed, and boy was that exciting.

Really exciting.

I didn't know anything about sex. Dad never breathed a word, and Mom couldn't bring herself to raise the topic. This was unchartered territory for both of us.

In the back of our property, there was a grassy corner hidden from the house. One night, we were passionately kissing each other, out of sight, when the clothes started flying off. Next thing we knew, we were doing the deed. I guess we figured out how things worked pretty quickly on our own.

I know I was her first, and she knew I had never been with a girl before.

I told her that I was going to be her husband, and she promised to become my wife. *And they call it puppy love.*

We did it a few more times. No protection, of course. I didn't even know what that was. But when the Beatles sang, "All you need is love," I now knew what they were singing about. When I heard the anti-war chants of "Make love, not war" on the nightly news, I was right there with the protesters.

I came of age in the late Sixties—a turbulent time in our history. Five years earlier—heck, make that three years earlier—a fourteen-year-old boy and a thirteen-year-old girl wouldn't have handed over their virginity so casually. But this was the era of hippies and free love when the social mores of the past were declared passé.

Mary Christine and I were swept up by that tide. To turn a popular phrase at the time, it felt right, so we did it.

TRYING OUT SOMETHING ELSE

A couple of weeks after the Woodstock music festival and its three days of sex, drugs, rock 'n' roll, and mud, I started my sophomore year at Notre Dame High.

This time around, I was looking forward to school because I wanted to try out for the JV basketball team in the fall. Playing two-on-two marathons in my driveway until 10 o'clock at night—as well as walking a few blocks to nearby Los Angeles Valley College on Saturday mornings for pick-up games all day long—really raised my game.

Basketball was my life. I even slept with my basketball because I heard my idol—Pistol Pete Maravich—did the same thing growing up. Pete was in his final year at Louisiana State University, scoring 44 points a game with a sleight-of-hand artistry that left crowds gasping and sportswriters crooning about the new sensation.

I practiced Pete's crossover and through-the-leg dribbles and bounced the basketball on one of the rails belonging to the railroad tracks that ran right next to the house. I even tried dribbling from a moving car while my mom drove down the street. I grew out my hair like Pete and wore his signature floppy socks and Converse Chuck Taylor All-Stars sneakers. I was militant about basketball.

I helped my cause by growing like a weed over the summer. I was no longer a pipsqueak with a future as a racehorse jockey. Going into my sophomore year, I was five feet, eight inches and still growing. Guard material.

I decided to try out for Notre Dame's B team, which was for fresh-man and sophomores. I didn't think I was good enough for the JV team, and there was no way I could play on varsity.

Basketball tryouts lasted two weeks. My heads-up play and excellent shooting raised the eyebrows of John Cicuto, the B team coach, who pen-ciled me at starting forward. He couldn't believe I had never played any organized ball before. I was on cloud nine. My stamina felt great. I barely used my inhaler because I felt I didn't need to.

Coach Cicuto scheduled a preseason practice at 8:30 a.m. one Satur-day morning. Before practice, I was eating a bowl of cereal at the kitchen table when my father walked in. This happened to be one of the week-ends he was home.

"Hey, don't you have practice today?" he asked. "You need to get going."

I clenched my teeth. Dad, telling me to go to practice—to do some-thing I had committed myself to doing. And he couldn't commit to being a full-time father.

I immediately rebelled. "We don't have practice today," I lied. Then I made a show of ignoring him and returning to my cereal.

Because I skipped practice, I had to quit the team. Coach Cicuto was more than surprised at my change of heart; he was actually upset. I made some cockamamie excuse about wanting to concentrate on my studies. Another lie. The reason I quit the basketball team was that I felt my father was forcing me into basketball—and I was going to do the opposite of what he wanted. I loved basketball, but once he injected himself into my life, I didn't want anything to do with him because of my hatred for who he was.

Then my little world was rocked by another calamity that fall.

Mary Christine stopped visiting me. She had started her freshman year at St. Genevieve's, a Catholic high school in nearby Panorama City, so naturally she was busy. Then her older sister Mary Lou dropped by one afternoon while I was shooting baskets in the driveway.

"I have some news for you," she said.

"Oh?"

"Yeah, Mary Christine has a new boyfriend."

My heart shot up into my throat. "Who?" I wondered.

"Andy Slimak, the freshman quarterback."

I was dumped for a football player. The devastating news was tough to swallow. I experienced my first broken heart, and it really hurt.

I vowed that wasn't going to happen again for a long time.

7

DAZED AND CONFUSED

I had another growth spurt during the summer between my sophomore and junior years. I shot up to five feet, eleven inches and finally felt like I belonged among my peers. I also got contacts, which meant I could ditch the nerdy glasses.

When school started in the fall, I was ready to settle some old scores. Mike Groff was a basketball player at Notre Dame who rode me unmercifully in the hallways and pick-up games, so he would be my first retaliation. On the first day of my junior year, I found him in the boys' locker room—and then I attacked. I pummeled him with my fists, knocked him to the ground, and then kicked him. "Don't you ever beat me up again!" I screamed.

I had a lot of anger boiling underneath the surface, and that stemmed from the home front. What happened is that toward the end of my sophomore year, I came home from school and found Mom in the living room, crying and devastated. To be honest, this was nothing out of the ordinary. I was heading toward my bedroom when—

"He's never coming back," she blurted.

I stopped in my tracks. "What do you mean he's never coming back?" I asked.

"We're getting a divorce."

Hearing her say that sent me into a tailspin. Mom was too upset to provide more details.

I remember trudging to my room. When you're a teenage boy, and your dad leaves your mom, it screws you up in the head. Even when my parents had big fights and my father would come and go as he pleased, I always held out hope that some day Dad would be a full-time father and always be around. But hearing Mom say that he wasn't coming back sounded like a death knell.

He was really gone. I had no idea where he was. No idea when I'd see him again. That's what I mean when I say it messes with your mind.

Playing basketball was like releasing a pressure valve of tension and worry. I started playing in summer leagues and continued practicing in my driveway. With Dad out of the picture, I felt like I was free to try out for the Notre Dame JV team that fall. This time around, I would be playing for myself. No father was reminding me to be on time for practice.

I was crazed and pumped up to make the JVs. For shooting drills, I shined above my competition. I made steals on defense. In team scrimmages, I led the floor in scoring. When we ran sprints at the end of practice, I beat everyone by twenty to twenty-five yards. I was the leader of the team, for all intents and purposes.

Mr. Nugent was the coach. Actually, he was a fill-in—an English teacher who didn't know basketball. I will never forget the afternoon when he posted a typewritten page listing those who made the team. My eyes scanned the names once, and then twice. Frank Sontag wasn't on it.

I was absolutely crushed. For nearly forty-five years, I've relived that moment a thousand times. Why did that have to happen? Didn't Mr. Nugent know I was the best shooter, the best dribbler, and the best defensive player on the team?

I didn't do a good job holding back my tears when I cornered the basketball coach and asked for an explanation. Mr. Nugent said the mission of the JV team at Notre Dame was to develop freshman and sophomores for the varsity team. Juniors were too old to play.

Too old? I was the same age as the sophomores!

Once again, the decision to have me skip fourth grade had shattering consequences on my life.

I could not give up the dream. Since Notre Dame was blocked, I played in city leagues because I had to play ball *somewhere*. On the school front, though, I was about as unmotivated as you could get. I was a solid 2.0 student who never applied himself and did enough to get by, except for chemistry, which I flunked. I had to take chemistry again during summer school before my junior year in 1971. This time around, I decided to make an effort. I took home an A. I excelled in math as well and loved algebra and trigonometry. I aced all my math tests without cracking open a textbook.

One primer I made sure I opened and read closely was the *California Driver Handbook*. I couldn't wait for my sixteenth birthday because that afforded me an opportunity to grab a golden ticket to freedom: a driver's license. Having my own wheels represented freedom—freedom from a broken home, freedom to hang out with my friends, and freedom to go wherever I wanted.

And freedom to attend rock 'n' roll concerts.

While my love for the Beatles hadn't diminished, they disbanded in the spring of 1970, which made me a free agent. Six months after the Beatles' break-up, Led Zeppelin became my new favorite band with the release of "Immigrant Song." This hard-driving, frenzied rock number was built around a repeating, staccato beat laid down by guitarist Jimmy Page, bassist John Paul Jones, and drummer John Bonham. Frontman Robert Plant opened the song with a distinctive, wailing cry that sent shivers down my spine.

When Led Zeppelin brought their North American tour to Los Angeles, I knew I had to be there. I had never been to a rock concert before, but that night at the Forum in Inglewood changed my life forever. Don't ask me how a couple of buddies and I scored center section seats in the third row, but it happened inside a sold-out arena filled with 18,000 screaming fans. When Jimmy Page busted out "Immigrant Song" as the opening number, I screamed like those teen girls at the *Ed Sullivan Show*. I had officially fallen in love with rock 'n' roll music.

My record collection added groups like Santana, Jethro Tull, Pink Floyd, the Allman Brothers Band, Deep Purple, Black Sabbath, and The Who. Now that the Beatles were no longer recording, I welcomed The Rolling Stones into my pantheon of bands, especially after the release of *Sticky Fingers* and its title track, "Brown Sugar," in the spring of 1971.

Mom was always harping on me to turn down the volume whenever I played the Stones or Led Zep in my bedroom; thus, music joined basketball in the center of my world. I wasn't interested in drinking beer or smoking marijuana, which made me unusual because *everybody* hit the keggers or smoked pot back then.

I remember hanging out at Carlos Miguel's house one time. A couple of our buddies were there. Carlos' bedroom was lined with blacklight posters, which were part of the psychedelic fashion scene. The fluorescent inks on the posters glowed when exposed to Carlos' ultraviolet lamp, which lit up his bedroom in a mood-altering way. Then he set a vinyl record on a Pioneer turntable. Black Sabbath's latest album, *Master of Reality*, started blasting away.

"Listen to this track," Carlos said. "It's called 'Sweet Leaf.' Know what's it about, Frank?"

The song began with someone coughing several times before the band launched into a typical heavy metal song—distorted power chords from an electric guitar punctuated by a thumping bass and drum beat.

I shrugged my shoulders. "What's the coughing about?" I asked.

Carlos and his buddies thought that was the funniest thing they'd heard in a long time. "That's Ozzy Osbourne coughing after he took a hit. 'Sweet Leaf' is about smoking doobies," Carlos said. "You're going to get high with us aren't you?" Then he reached for a baggie containing a stash of marijuana.

"Sorry, but no way and no how," I said. "I'm a basketball player."

My friends knew how crazy I was for hoops and how I got a raw deal at Notre Dame, but that didn't stop them from getting on my case.

"You can still smoke. What's your problem, man?" one of my friends wondered. "Don't you want to be cool?"

All three friends laid down a thick spread of peer pressure, even calling me a square, which was a stronger pejorative than it is today. I didn't budge. I was an athlete trying to keep the dream alive. I knew pot and sports weren't a good mix.

Basketball—and music—were the only things I focused on during my high school years. My friends knew I didn't drink and didn't date either. I swore off girls after Mary Christine dumped me.

And then I found something else that captured my interest: earning money.

PART-TIME WORK

There was another reason I couldn't wait for my sixteenth birthday on July 6, 1971, that went beyond getting my driver's license. Turning sixteen meant I could work part-time, and I wanted a job so that I could pay for the gas, insurance, and upkeep of an old Fiat that my parents gave me for my Sweet Sixteen birthday. Dad showed up sporadically, and I knew

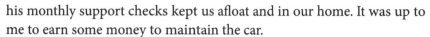

his monthly support checks kept us afloat and in our home. It was up to me to earn some money to maintain the car.

I talked to my best friend, Barry Traub, about what I should do.

"You don't want to work at McDonald's," Barry said.

"Why not?" Back then, there were just a handful of fast food chains. I figured I had to work for Ronald McDonald, flipping burgers.

"They'll start you on the fries line, and it's the worst job. You go home smelling like French fry grease. That's if you're lucky enough to not burn yourself with hot oil. I got a better job for you."

"What's that?"

"Ralphs supermarket, boxing groceries."

I could do that. Sounded a lot safer—and less smelly—than working next to a hot, greasy fryer.

The day after I celebrated my sixteenth birthday with a successful trip to the Department of Motor Vehicles, I stepped into the Ralphs in Sherman Oaks on the corner of Ventura and Woodman and filled out an application. I was hired on the spot at minimum wage: $1.92 an hour.

My job title was box boy. I was told there was an art to bagging groceries and I needed to learn it. You square up your brown paper bag—no plastic sacks in those days—and drop in the heavy stuff first: the cans of spaghetti sauce, jars of pickles, half-gallons of ice cream, and gallons of milk. I had to make sure I put square items in each corner and filled in from there. The lighter products—boxed cereals, crackers, and starches like rice and beans—filled in the gaps. Light produce, like lettuce and parsley, landed on top.

When I helped little old ladies by wheeling their groceries out to the car, I'd be offered a quarter tip, but I held to Ralphs' code of ethics—no gratuities. "Thanks, ma'am, but that won't be necessary," I'd say. "Thank you for coming to Ralphs."

Instead of seeing box boy as a dead end job, I embraced it. My quick hands on the basketball court translated well. I nimbly scooped up foodstuffs flying off the conveyor belt and filled the brown bags lickety-split. It was all about service. I even liked working two check stands at a time, bouncing back and forth like a basketball guard on a full-court press.

My store manager noticed my hustle. After being with Ralphs for half a year, my boss nominated me for the "Box Boy of the Year" competition held annually among the Ralphs stores in the L.A. region. In this contest, they'd have the same groceries waiting at each check stand, and then a clerk would send the items down the conveyer belt. Box boys—and girls, I might add—were timed for speed and accuracy as well as form and fit inside the brown paper bags. I'm telling you, this was our Olympics.

I won a district competition, which qualified me for the finals—at my store! It seems that the Ralphs supermarket in Sherman Oaks was the largest and most successful in the company, so home-court advantage for me. The finalists could choose their checkout stand, which turned out to be a big break. I knew the conveyor belt on check stand 3 was the fastest one.

That's not why I won "Box Boy of the Year." I like to think it was because of my exceptional hand-eye coordination, my superb judgment on which food items went into the bag first, and my superior packing skills. All I know is that I took a lot of pride in winning, which netted me a trophy and a monetary award. I got a wage bump to $2.02 an hour, a ten-cent-an-hour raise that felt like a million bucks to a sixteen-year-old kid.

I was working eighteen, twenty hours a week—three evenings a week from 3 p.m. to 7 p.m. and an eight-hour shift on Saturday or Sunday. I had money to spend, and I liked that feeling.

It's funny, but to this day I don't let anybody bag my groceries.

A TURN AWAY

At Notre Dame, I was taught by the Brothers of the Congregation of the Holy Cross, who founded the high school in 1947. These religious brothers, who were not ordained like priests were, nonetheless took vows of poverty, celibacy, and obedience. Some dressed in a casual shirt and slacks, but most wore black Cossacks and Roman collars, so they looked the part of a religious order.

Maintaining classroom discipline wasn't easy in an all-boys high school fueled with testosterone, which stoked aggressive and mean behavior. I witnessed the latter when Brother Dobrogowski lost control of one of my classes. It seemed that Brother DoBro, as we called him in the school yard, served our country in World War II as an infantryman. We heard he had shellshock problems, or what they call post-traumatic stress syndrome (PTSD) today.

Some of the kids in my class thought it would be funny if they pantomimed pulling the pin on a grenade, tossing it in Brother Dobrogowski's direction, then ducking underneath their desks and making the sounds of explosions. I confess to joining in the jocularity.

Poor Brother Dobrogowski. It wasn't long after that he suffered a nervous breakdown and had to leave the school. That's what good Catholic boys we were in those days.

It's during my time at Notre Dame that I stopped identifying myself as a member of the faith. When things got crazy after Dad left, we quit fulfilling our holy day of obligation on Sunday mornings (or Saturday nights) at St. Francis de Sales. Where was God in the midst of all my pain anyway?

I was tired of hearing about Catholic dogma and the infallibility of the Pope at Notre Dame. That, coupled with working at Ralphs on Saturday or Sunday, or sometimes both days, gave me a convenient excuse to skip Mass. As far as I was concerned, that's all she wrote. Once I graduated from Notre Dame, I was never going back to the Catholic Church.

Until I walked with my class, I had to hang in there. Religion was a mandatory class each semester, but I don't recall ever reading the Bible in the classroom or as part of a homework assignment. Nor were we shown how Scripture could be applied to how we should live or conduct ourselves. Instead, we studied the do's and don'ts found in the *Baltimore Catechism* or learned about saints such as St. Michael the Archangel or St. Christopher, the patron saint of travel whose name was invoked by mariners for safety.

Religion class was always taught by a brother, but at the start of my senior year, a layman was assigned to fill the minds of twenty boys with more Catholic mush. His name was Mr. LaPlante.

One morning, Mr. LaPlante held up a color painting of Jesus walking through a shepherd's meadow, surrounded by a flock of sheep and with a cute white lamb wrapped around the back of his shoulders.

"No doubt, you've seen this illustration of Jesus carrying a lamb on his shoulders," Mr. LaPlante began. "This is evidence that Jesus Christ was gay."

The room froze.

Yes, Mr. LaPlante used the word *gay*, which was rarely uttered in the early '70s. Today, the use of *gay* is commonplace, and the three-letter word has a universal meaning for males: if someone is gay, that means he's a homosexual. Back then, however, the word *gay* was more nuanced. It *could* mean you preferred to have sexual relations with men, but more often it meant you were effeminate.

In other words, what Mr. LaPlante was saying, or at least how I understood it as a sixteen-year-old, was that Jesus was a pansy—someone "light in his loafers" as we used to say in the locker room. To say someone was "light in his loafers" meant he was light on his feet, someone who minced around like a ballet dancer.

Okay, so we're parsing words here. Looking back through the prism of time, I'm sure Mr. LaPlante meant to say that the Son of God was a homosexual, which was an outrageous and untrue statement—and a horrible lie to make in front of a class of impressionable teenage minds.

Two days later, we had a new religion teacher. A couple of students had told their parents, who immediately called the principal, and Mr. LaPlante no longer had a job teaching at Notre Dame.

But the damage was done. Think about it: I can still recall this incident—and Pete LaPlante's full name—more than forty years later. If this memory is as vivid to me as my bald head, what about the effect his proclamation had on my fellow classmates?

As far as I was concerned, that was one more huge red flag with religion. The incident with Mr. LaPlante reminded me of the taunts and jibes I had received.

Hey Son-of-a-fag!

Even graduating from high school a year ahead of schedule wasn't early enough.

8

SCHOOL'S OUT

I don't recall meeting with a school counselor about my plans after high school. There was no need to. A four-year college wasn't on the horizon.

My SAT score confirmed that I wasn't cut out for the rigors of academia. I posted an 820 back in the day when a perfect score was 1600. (It's 2400 today.) Not stellar at all. According to SAT's statistics, 80 percent of students scored better than me.

I'm not sure if I was mature enough to handle a four-year university anyway. I was still sixteen when I walked with the Class of '72 at Notre Dame, a month shy of my seventeenth birthday. Feeling very unsettled and unsure about my future, I sorely lacked a year of maturation.

As I touched on before, I was painted into this academic corner by a fourth grade teacher who recommended to my parents that I skip a school year. I paid a steep price for that suggestion. What happened in classrooms for the next seven grades was a disaster. There's no other way to describe it. My extracurricular activities took a hit as well. Because I got a late start playing basketball and lacked physical maturity during my freshman and sophomore years, I never got untracked on the court. Socially, I was bullied and belittled in hallways and locker rooms. At the end of the day, what a wasted opportunity at a time when the world should have been my oyster.

In no way do I blame my parents. Undoubtedly, they were proud as peacocks when told that their kid was so smart that he deserved to be accelerated a grade level. "Teacher knows best" was the phrase I heard growing up. These days, the practice of skipping a grade is far less common, thanks to the development of gifted student curriculum and Advanced Placement courses in high school. But looking back, my childhood passed by in a blur. What was the rush anyway?

The only constant in my life was basketball. I couldn't give up the game, not even after I tried out my senior year at Notre Dame and had the most humiliating experience ever. I was trying to elbow my way onto the varsity team, my only option as a senior. One last shot.

Three days into tryouts, we were playing a team scrimmage—referees, scoreboard, everything. I was sitting at the end of the bench, not expecting to play. I was last on the depth chart, remember? With two minutes to go in a blowout game, though, I heard my name called.

"Get in there, Sontag," the head coach growled.

I hustled to the scorer's table to check in. I was taking off my sweat pants when I realized I didn't have any basketball shorts on. Just a jockstrap.

I immediately pulled up my sweat pants. Play stopped, and the referee signaled for me to come in. I jogged onto the court and played the last two minutes of the game wearing navy blue sweat pants. Everyone *knew* what happened. My greatest wish was to die immediately—or at least fall through a hole in the gym floor.

It didn't take long for word to get around an all-boys school that Sontag forgot to put his shorts on. Mercifully, I got cut from the team shortly thereafter.

I eventually recovered from the disgrace and joined a pair of city leagues that played on weeknights. Following graduation, I got into a couple of high-level summer leagues. I also played pick-up games at schoolyards and nearby Valley College, more than holding my own against seasoned players. I may not have had any high school playing experience, but I had plenty of street basketball in my game.

As for what I was going to do in the fall, I knew junior college was my only option. As I treaded water and considered what to do, I upped my hours at Ralphs. I liked earning money, and receiving a paycheck every Friday did loads for my sagging self-esteem.

A couple of guys I knew at Notre Dame told me they were trying out for the basketball team at Valley College, which was a two-year community college. I knew I was as good as they were. If they were trying out, why shouldn't I?

Valley College was easy to get into. If you could fog a mirror, you were in. I think my tuition fees were less than $100.

I trained as never before for basketball tryouts during the fall of 1972. I thought I had a great camp. Made my shots. Hustled on defense. Showed some court savvy.

Thirty players participated in the tryouts. After a week, the Valley coach, Gaston Green, had everyone sit on the floor.

"When I call your name, give me your shoe size," said Coach Green, an African-American who came to Valley from Freemont High in South-Central L.A. While at Fremont, he had coached Curtis Rowe, who went on to play on three NCAA national championship teams at UCLA under legendary coach John Wooden. Coach Green knew his way around a hardcourt.

When Coach said he wanted shoe sizes, the players looked around at each other, wondering what this was all about. As Coach Green called out names, I got it: He was naming those who made the team! I held my breath . . . hoping . . . wishing . . . and then I heard him say, "Sontag."

I almost wanted to leap to my feet and kiss my first black man. Instead, I grinned and said, "Eleven-and-a-half, Coach." Then the magnitude of what happened hit me in the chest. I had finally made a team. I fought back tears—just barely.

A week or two later, Coach Green stopped me after practice. "Frank, we really love your abilities," he began.

Uh-oh. I waited for the *but*.

"But I just found out you're seventeen years old. Would you consider redshirting for a year?"

I had no idea what redshirting signified. "What do you mean, Coach?"

Coach Green explained that redshirting happens when an athlete is kept out of college competition and allowed to develop without using up a year of eligibility. "You'll still practice on the team, but the year doesn't count," Coach said. "You'll come back next season as a freshman and be caught up age-wise."

I agreed to his plan for me to sit out a year and practice with the team.

After a couple of weeks, a few guys made it real clear that I didn't belong any longer. They were vicious in how they knocked me around the court and made nasty comments when Coach was out of earshot. I wasn't in their clique.

I couldn't put up with that for the next three months. I had a meeting with Coach Green and told him I was thinking about quitting the team and playing City League ball.

"I don't like the idea," Coach responded. "You'll be better off practicing with the team. But if that's what you want to do, then it's up to you."

I left the team. The following summer, I played on Valley's summer league team and did really, really well. All signs were pointing toward a banner freshman season. I had filled out and grown taller. I stood at six feet, three inches, good height for a shooting guard or small forward.

Then, just before the season started, Coach Green left Valley College for greener coaching pastures. (In case you recognize his name, his son, Gaston Green III, turned out to be a standout running back at UCLA and played six years in the NFL.)

His replacement, Doug Michaelson, didn't like me. I don't know what I said or what I had done, but we didn't gel. After the first week of practice, he cut me. "I want nothing to do with you," Coach Michaelson said in parting.

Nice guy.

There wasn't much point to remaining in school. I'm not sure if I finished the semester or dropped out of Valley College immediately.

It didn't matter. No one wanted me to play basketball.

STANDING IN

Meanwhile, I was still living at home. Mom liked having me around because she was alone, and I liked keeping my expenses down. After Dad filed for divorce, Mom went to beauty college so that she could become a licensed hairdresser. She had dropped out of high school at sixteen to marry Dad, so she didn't have anything to fall back on.

Since I was no longer a student, I threw myself into the grocery industry. My bosses at Ralph's had always liked me, so they were happy to see me up my hours to full-time status. My days as a box boy were over. I became a checkstand clerk and also worked night crew, stocking shelves.

After a while on night crew, I got the bug to start moving up. In the fall of 1974, I was offered the position of assistant grocery manager, the bottom rung of management, at the Ralphs on 3rd and La Brea north of the Wilshire district, not far from downtown L.A.

For someone just nineteen years old, this was a huge break. "We think you're managerial material," one confided. "You can make a career out of the supermarket industry."

Shortly after this promotion, my father contacted me. We stayed in loose contact after he left the house and the marriage for good.

Mom and I had learned why Dad was disappearing all those years: he had been having an affair with the receptionist at our family doctor's office. She was a widow with two children, having lost her husband to cancer. In every sense of the phrase, Dad had been living the proverbial double life.

Anita was her name. When Dad brought her to one of my city league games and introduced me, I liked her. She seemed like a very sweet person.

This time around, Dad contacted me because the divorce had been finalized. "I'm planning to marry Anita. Would you be my best man and stand in for us?" he asked.

I said yes because I loved my dad. You talk about a walking contradiction. There was still a wounded part of me that sought my dad's love, and I imagined there was a part of him that loved his son as well. I told him I would be pleased to be his best man when he married Anita in a civil ceremony before a justice of the peace. The marriage date was February 21, 1975—Anita's birthday.

We went out for dinner afterwards, and Dad asked me how I liked working at Ralphs. I told him I absolutely loved it and thought I found my sweet spot in life. I got a kick out the people I worked with and enjoyed helping the locals who shopped for groceries.

At Ralphs La Brea, I worked the swing shift from 5 p.m. until 2 a.m. Crazy things happened at night. We had a fortyish-old woman who regularly came into the store at dinner time. She was a big-name actress in a popular TV series and quite friendly. After several visits, I could tell she had it out for me. She was a cougar on the prowl.

One night she called Ralphs and asked to speak with a manager, knowing I was on duty. I recognized the voice.

"Hi, Frank. I was wondering if you could bring me a few things."

"Sure, Mrs. Robinson." (That's not her real name, but it seems appropriate.)

"I need a dozen eggs, butter, some lox and bagels, and a bottle of whiskey. Can you deliver?"

"Of course," I replied. I was Mr. Can Do, and we did delivery at our store.

I took down her address and promised to be there in twenty minutes. When I knocked, she opened the door—and was wearing only a smile. She was totally naked.

"Come on in," she purred. "I've been waiting for you."

"I'm . . . I'm . . . I'm not sure that's a good idea, Mrs. Robinson. I have to get back to the store."

"Oh, don't be ridiculous. No one will miss you."

That wasn't the point. I handed her the bag of groceries and got out of there as quickly as I could. I also had a good story to tell the guys in the break room.

There was another story that I shared with my co-workers, but this one happened at home. Since I worked until 2 a.m., I usually didn't get home until 3 in the morning. I often made myself a sandwich and then went to bed and would sleep until noon.

One morning at 9 a.m., the phone next to my bed jangled me out of a deep sleep. I groggily answered. It was one of the Johnson girls next door.

"Frank, there are some suspicious-looking people hiding in the bushes on your property," she said.

I was instantly awake. Two days earlier, we had a home-invasion burglary. Seems I had the left the house to run an errand during the day, and when I came back, the front door was busted wide open. Glass in the door was broken and in shards.

With the front door ajar, a burglar or burglars could still be in the house. I ran next door to the Johnsons to call the police.

A squad car arrived shortly. Two cops jumped out and drew their weapons. I described the layout of the house. Then they entered the house and looked around. When they returned, one said, "The house is clear. Sorry, but your place has been ransacked, especially your bedroom."

My hopes were raised. My bedroom was always ransacked. I was a slob. Maybe nothing of value was taken.

"They also hit your mom's bedroom and bathroom. Looks like they got everything of value."

The burglars stole Mom's jewelry and silver coin collection from her father, as well as our silverware. All told, we lost several thousand dollars in personal items, but the sentimental cost was much higher.

And now, two days later, some sketchy-looking transients were hiding behind our property wall. After thanking the Johnson girl for the tip, I hopped out of bed and put on some shorts over my boxers. Then I tiptoed to a picture window in the front and peered from behind the curtains. My next-door neighbor had been right. Those were creepy-looking people hiding in our bushes. Two guys and a gal. They were crouched behind our cinder block property wall in such a way that they would not be seen from the street.

I slipped back to my room and opened a closet door. A 12-gauge shotgun stood in a corner. I reached for the firearm and pumped the action to double-check that there were no shells. I did not want to take a loaded weapon out front. I just wanted to take control of the situation.

Then I picked up the phone and called next door. "Call the police now!" I told the Johnson girl.

I stepped out the front door, wearing only shorts, shotgun raised. I hunched low and crouched closer. When I felt like I was the right distance away, I stood up and took aim. "Freeze! Don't move!"

They looked very surprised to see the barrel of a 12-gauge shotgun pointed at them. They quickly raised their hands. I was thinking of what I should do next when I heard a police chopper sweep overhead. No one moved. Then two black-and-whites pulled into the driveway.

Cops jumped out, but instead of training their pistols on the intruders, they directed their weapons at me.

"Put the gun down!" one yelled.

"I live here!" I screamed back.

"Put the gun down!"

I did as ordered. Next thing I knew I was being rough-handled to the front lawn, where I was ordered to lay down in the grass face-first.

"Hands to the back!" a cop ordered.

I was handcuffed, all the while protesting my treatment. "I live here!" I cried out.

One of the girls next door vouched for me. I was released from the handcuffs. The three others were not so fortunate. It turned out that a half hour earlier, they had robbed a house in the neighborhood and were trying to beat a manhunt by hiding behind our property wall. The stolen goods were in their roller suitcases, so the cops had them dead to rights.

As the police led the three 'cuffed suspects to a squad car, another officer returned my 12-gauge. Before handing the firearm over, he pumped the action to eject any shells.

"Your shotgun's empty," he said.

"I know."

One of the suspects overheard the conversation as he was being led to a black and white for transport to county jail. "You held us with an empty gun? I'm going to come back and kill you."

I didn't answer him back. Instead, I watched as the cops took him away. All in all, it was an exciting morning for a twenty-year-old. This is what I lived for—an exhilarating life.

I was invincible.

MOVING UP THE LADDER

Ralphs was an innovative Southern California chain that established some of the first full-scale supermarkets in the early 1920s as well as a six-rung managerial ladder. The progression looked like this:

- No. 1: store manager
- No. 2: assistant manager
- No. 3: grocery manager
- No. 4: checkstand manager
- No. 5: assistant checkstand manager
- No. 6: assistant grocery manager

After two years, I was promoted from assistant grocery manager (No. 6) to checkstand manager (No. 4) at Ralphs La Brea, which was unheard of at the company. You usually move up just one position every two or three years, but my superiors thought I deserved the double promotion.

One of my new responsibilities included arresting shoplifters. When someone walked in and acted suspiciously—like forgoing a shopping cart or hand basket or wearing a heavy raincoat on a sunny day in July—I'd make my way to the back of the store and mount a set of stairs to a catwalk that overlooked the floor. Two-way mirrors assured that no one could see me behind the glass.

Sure enough, a heavyset woman in her thirties arrived wearing a thick overcoat. It hadn't rained in months.

When she lingered next to the meat case—without a cart or a basket—I knew where this was going. I watched her slip New York cuts, porterhouse steaks, and packs of tenderloins into the inner pockets of her overcoat. She looked around to make sure she wasn't being watched, but she had no idea I was studying every movement from behind the mirrored glass.

When she slipped out of the store, I was waiting for her in the parking lot—with handcuffs. I calmly explained that I had seen her steal the meat—and 'cuffed her before she could run off. I led her to a back room and called the police. When a pair of LAPD patrolmen arrived, a pat down revealed that she had boosted eighty-five pounds of USDA prime cuts inside her raincoat. As they led her out of the store, one cop told me she was a druggie who stole expensive steaks to sell on the black market. "It's all about the next fix," he said.

Dealing with shoplifters was far less dangerous than dealing with armed robbers. Most of the time the bandits leveled a handgun at a clerk, cleaned out a cash register, and ran off with a couple of hundred bucks. The only redeeming factor was that the hold-ups were over quickly.

Ralphs La Brea wasn't open twenty-four hours a day; we closed at 1 a.m. Sometime around eight o'clock one evening, a disheveled guy with straggly brown hair and bearded stubble walked in dressed in a cowboy shirt and blue jeans. He approached me at the main checkstand.

"What time do you close?" he asked. His manner was brusque, not friendly.

"We're open till one o'clock in the morning," I politely responded. It seemed like an odd question to ask since closing time was five hours away.

He walked around the store, not carrying a basket or pushing a cart. Even Inspector Clouseau could see that he wasn't in the store to pick up a gallon of milk and a loaf of bread. He was casing the joint. I cast a wary eye and did my best not to draw attention to myself. I thought he was going to hit one of our cash registers when the timing was right, but he abruptly left the store instead. He walked outside, where someone—an accomplice, I figured—was waiting for him in a car.

I called the Los Angeles Police Department and reached the watch commander at the Wilshire division. When I described the situation, he patched me into his superior—a lieutenant who ran the show.

I identified myself as the night manager at Ralphs and said someone suspicious had come into the store a few minutes earlier. I described the incident and what the suspect looked like.

"Let me call you back." The gravelly voice was all business.

When I heard back from the lieutenant, he had a question for me.

"Would you have any reservations about having a SWAT team come to the store?"

"No. Of course not."

A SWAT team on the premises would liven up a dull day selling groceries. I was all for bringing the men in blue in.

"Do you have a receiving dock in the back?" the lieutenant asked.

"Yes, we do."

"Look for a white Matador to pull up. That'll be the guys. Let them in."

Twenty minutes later, a two-door AMC sedan drove up to the rear of the store. Six SWAT guys in full gear—tactical vests, helmets, modular knee pads, leather boots, all in black—popped out of that Matador like they were Marines going to war. They were serious. It looked like a movie scene.

The head guy spoke in crisp, military cadence. "Do you have blueprints to the store?"

"Yeah. I can find them."

"Then get 'em."

I quickly rounded up the blueprints and spread them out on a desk in Receiving. Orders were issued to set up a perimeter and change into plain clothes. I watched the elite policemen take off their tactical uniforms and don T-shirts and jeans, followed by light jackets. The first thing that caught my eye were all the guns strapped to their legs. They also had semi-automatic weapons holstered around their chests.

I was wondering what precipitated the ramp-up in police force. Before I could ask, the lead guy explained the mission. "There are two hardened criminals we have to take down. They've robbed several stores and killed two people. They're armed and dangerous."

"Whoa, I didn't know this was that serious."

Then he had another question. "Do you have a catwalk?"

I led him up and showed him the lay of the land. There was an exit at each end of the store. One was next to the Liquor department. The other was near the last checkstand.

The cop in charge leaned closer and pointed toward the exit next to the Liquor department. "If they take you hostage, the moment the doors kick open, fall to the floor. We'll waste them."

I nearly lost my dinnertime *carne asada* burrito when I heard that.

The next thing I heard is that he wanted to wire me. I got hooked up with an earpiece.

"You look really nervous," the head cop said as he finished fitting me. "They're probably not coming in before midnight, so stay calm. Do your work. Frank, we're professionals. We will kill these guys on sight. Don't worry."

I was momentarily reassured, but we were all on heightened alert inside the store as the midnight hour neared. Every time one of the entrance doors opened, my heart rate shot up. I was a nervous wreck. I was thinking that maybe I had been a little too cavalier a few hours earlier. I didn't want to die. Certainly not this way.

From the main checkout stand, I saw guys walking around with carts who didn't look like shoppers. They were SWAT team members in plain clothes, tough-looking dudes. Elite police personnel.

Three were positioned inside the store. Another one out front; one in the back. The lead cop moved about, skittish as a cat.

As the clock neared the 1 a.m. closing, my nervousness ratcheted up four notches. "It's zero hour," said the voice in my earpiece. "If they're going to do it, it'll happen in the next ten minutes."

Those were the longest ten minutes in my life.

One a.m. came and passed without incident, however. I breathed a heavy sigh of relief as I locked up. Then I saw familiar faces coming my way—the night crew. They were, for the most part, sloppy-looking guys who threw cans on the shelves in the middle of the night.

One of them was a real character—an Armenian guy named Tiny Nalbanian. He was built like a butterball turkey and weighed 300 pounds, hence the nickname "Tiny."

Tiny and his cohorts started filtering in, not suspecting a thing. I was counting my register when Tiny walked by.

"Give me all your money," he joked.

No sooner had he got the word *money* out of his mouth when four guns were pointed at his head.

The look on Tiny's face was priceless.

I threw out my arms. "No, no, he's one of us. He's night crew. He's okay."

Tiny had no idea what had just gone down.

After that incident, the SWAT team cleared the store. They didn't find anyone.

Three nights later, the two robbers knocked off a Safeway in the area. One of the criminals killed a store employee during the commission of a robbery. A SWAT team responded and shot and killed one of the criminals.

I was sobered by the news. I could have been that dead employee.

It took me several months to shake off the incident. Overall, though, I was happy at Ralphs La Brea. Our supermarket was smaller than most Ralphs and fit me like a comfortable glove. But Ralphs' policy was to promote from within every two years. By 1977, I'd been with Ralphs La Brea for two-and-a-half years, so corporate was looking to move me up a level to No. 3—grocery manager—at a new store.

I was told that my new assignment would be the Ralphs supermarket on Sunset Boulevard in West Hollywood. This was a flagship store, one of the Top 5 in Southern California in terms of volume. In career terms, this was a super big promotion for me. Basically, I'd be the guy who ran the night crew, working the graveyard shift from midnight to 9 a.m.

Little did I know that the craziness was about to begin.

9

WON'T GET
FOOLED AGAIN

For someone just twenty-one years old, the promotion to the full-ser-vice, 50,000-square-foot Ralphs on Sunset Boulevard, open 24/7, was a vivid sign that I was moving up the ladder.

The supermarket was a zoo on Friday and Saturday nights. Remember, this was the heart of Hollywood during the height of the disco era, circa 1977. John Travolta wannabes flooded the streets wearing white polyester two-button single-breasted suits with wide lapels and flared trousers, while their dance partners wore shimmery dresses and chunky jewelry. After grooving to the Bee Gees in the trendy discotheques that populated the Strip, they'd take the party home, which necessitated a stop at Ralphs. No wonder booze and snack foods were our big money makers.

Bottles of Southern Comfort, Smirnoff, and Bacardi, bags of Lay's Potato Chips and Fritos Corn Chips, and every salty snack you can think of filled shopping carts. The checkstands were backed up between the hours of midnight and 2 a.m. Everyone was busy. I supervised the cashiers and ran the night crew that restocked shelves, but half the time we were dealing with alcohol-induced collapses and cleaning up vomit on Aisle 4.

Prostitutes roamed Sunset in thickets. I can remember a couple of hookers, with gold lamé miniskirts hiked up their thighs, teetering in on five-inch platform heels and making a beeline to the Health and Beauty Aids aisle where, I kid you not, they dropped their red thongs and cleaned themselves with feminine hygiene products. They didn't care who saw them.

We were known as "Rock 'n' Roll Ralphs" because we were close to the Guitar Center on the Sunset Strip and because rock stars and movie celebrities dropped in at all hours of the night. They either had the munchies, or they were making a booze run. Or both.

One time after midnight, I passed the magazine rack that was stacked with the latest issue of *People* magazine. Fleetwood Mac was on the cover; they were huge in 1977 because of a trio of hit songs on their *Fleetwood Mac* album: "Over My Head," "Rhiannon," and "Say You Love Me."

And then the entire band walked into Rock 'n' Roll Ralphs, which created a scene. Things were cool until an incident developed at one of the checkstands. Stevie Nicks, the lead singer, wanted to cash a check for $500, which needed my approval.

"How can I help?" I asked the rock goddess.

"Your @#$% clerk won't cash my @#$% check."

Stevie was slurring her words. She was pretty drunk.

"Stevie, I can't cash your check. I'd love to help, but I can't do it." My personal limit was $100.

"You @#$%." She left the store in a huff, the longhaired band members trailing in her wake.

It's amazing how fast the craziness surrounding Rock 'n' Roll Ralphs started to feel normal. I'd been at the store for a month when I was perched behind the manager's desk one evening. My workstation faced the dozen checkstands. This is where the manager on duty kept an eye on things and—in those days before the widespread use of credit and debit cards—was called upon to approve checks. Behind me, to my immediate right and left, shelves of liquor were stacked with popular brands of whiskey, vodka, rum, and just about every hard spirit you could name. Remember, we had a diverse clientele to serve—and liquor sales padded our bottom line.

Suddenly, I heard the sound of breaking glass and then *plink, plink, plink*. I instinctively ducked for cover as bottles of whiskey to my right exploded into chards and the brown liquid sprayed everywhere. Screams of fright filled the busy store as customers and clerks sought cover.

I looked up—and saw the gunman standing next to the skylight above my workstation. He was on our roof. We made eye contact. Then he shouldered a light rifle and took off.

I quickly called 911. The LAPD was very active on Sunset, so there were always cops on patrol. Two black-and-whites were in our parking lot in no more than a minute or two. I ran out and explained that a gunman had apparently gotten on our roof, shot through a skylight, and taken several potshots into the store.

One of the cops radioed for help, and a perimeter was set up. The policemen caught the dude climbing down a fire escape ladder at the rear of the store. Turned out some crazed guy, sky high on drugs, thought it would be fun to squeeze off a few rounds, using glass bottles of Southern Comfort and Johnny Walker Red for target practice. That's why there was a *plink* each time he discharged his .22 caliber rifle.

Upper management didn't tell me that part of my job description at Rock 'n' Roll Ralphs would include being shot at—or filling out tons of police reports for grab-and-go hold-ups, shoplifting, and belligerent drunks. There was never an ordinary night in a store where you never knew what would happen next.

One night after I'd been at Rock 'n' Roll Ralphs for a couple of months, I was helping the night crew restock. My guys came in at midnight and started in Receiving, where they filled big steel bins with the latest shipment of foodstuffs that had arrived earlier in the day.

We set up a big cutting board inside the store, next to one of the walls in the meat department. This was an assembly line: two guys pulled cases of food out of the steel bins, which they slid down the table. Next, two guys with box cutters sliced open the boxes and slid them on to the next pair, who "marked" each canned good or boxed item with a price tag from a marking stick. In the late '70s, we were just starting to switch over to scanning technology.

Once each piece of merchandise was marked, two guys tossed the boxes onto "two wheelers"—tables that moved the stacks of goods to the appropriate aisles or endcaps, where popular foods such as carbonated sodas, savory snack items, and sweet bakery items were highly visible. Some endcaps were a good deal for the customer—we called them loss leaders—and some were a good deal for us.

We were working the long cutting board when multiple sirens split the night. This was nothing unusual for busy Sunset Boulevard on a

Saturday night, when the cops were always responding to distress calls or chasing bad guys. On this particular evening, one siren got louder and louder, so blaring it sounded like a cop car was coming right into our—

The entrance doors suddenly kicked open, and a desperate-looking man—looking over his shoulder—burst into the store. He immediately turned and started sprinting for his life, tearing goods off the shelves. He darted past the produce section and careened toward us in the meat department at the rear of the store.

At the same time, I heard the screech of slamming brakes. What happened next was straight out of an action flick: a black-and-white rammed through the front entrance, sending glass and steel everywhere in a cloud of smoke. Two cops jumped out, pistols drawn. The next thing I knew, shots were fired, and my buddies and I hit the linoleum floor. The suspect rushed past as more police gunfire rang out. He smashed through the black rubber swivel doors separating the store from Receiving.

We stayed low as the cops gave chase. No more shots were fired.

In the distance, I heard a commanding voice bark, "Get down!"

The suspect was captured in the back. A minute later, a couple of cops returned to let us know that the coast was clear. He was apprehended on the loading dock by other units responding to the call. Apparently, this guy had robbed Du-pars, a comfort food diner on the Strip that was similar to Denny's or Coco's. The stick-up went south when he shot an employee, which raised the stakes. Hence the speedy chase.

Apologies were made for busting through our front entrance, and there were grocery items all over the floor from the mad dash by the suspect, who grabbed at boxes and cans during his flight. We had quite a clean-up on hand, and I had more police reports to fill out. We also discovered stray bullets in some of our pot roasts.

The crazy behavior I encountered at Rock 'n' Roll Ralphs started to get to me. The shootings, the prostitutes, the druggies, and the party animals—what a circus. We had a homeless encampment behind the store where down-and-outers injected their arms with heroin. Many of them dumpster-dived to feed themselves.

A song getting a lot of airtime in the summer of 1977 was "Take This Job and Shove It" by Johnny Paycheck. I didn't listen to country music—I was a rock guy—but the song's title became a catchphrase in the culture. Perhaps that was the tipping point to quit my job, free as a bird. At least I wouldn't have to duck bullets in that madhouse any longer. After three months in Rock 'n' Roll Ralphs, six nights a week, I decided I couldn't do it anymore.

One morning, I walked up to store manager Jim Loyola at the manager's desk. Seeing him there reminded me of the shower of glass when bottles of hard spirits exploded from .22 rounds.

"Boss, I'm quitting," I announced. "I'm done. This is my last day. I can't do this. This is insanity."

I placed my keys on his desk.

Jim's square jaw dropped. "You can't just walk out."

"Watch me."

I was on a flight later that afternoon to Portland, Oregon. I had a friend who attended the University of Oregon in Eugene, and there was a standing invitation to come visit. I didn't feel safe in L.A., so I wanted to get out of town.

I picked up a rental car in Portland and headed south. I caught up with my friend in Eugene and loved the ivy-covered brick walls on the U of O campus. Then I drove over to Coos Bay on the coast to see where Steve Prefontaine grew up. "Pre," as he was known before his untimely death two years earlier, was America's greatest distance runner and was an icon in the world of track. He, along with Pistol Pete Maravich, were my favorite heroes because they were counter-cultural—ran their own races, as it were.

I liked Oregon. "God's country," they called it. Tall firs. Rugged coastline. Green alfalfa valleys. I liked the Beaver State so much that I dropped by Chemeketa Community College in Salem, the state capitol, to inquire about trying out for the basketball team. I wasn't impulsive or wounded or anything.

I talked to the coach, toured the facilities, and liked what I saw. Then I went to the admissions department and filled out all the necessary paperwork to enroll at Chemeketa.

I flew home after three vagabond weeks in Oregon. The idea of pulling up stakes and moving more than 1,000 miles to Salem looked different when viewed through the lens of reality back in L.A. Logically, it didn't make sense to make such a big move when I wasn't sure if I'd make a junior college basketball team. It wouldn't be cheap to move, plus I'd be paying out-of-state tuition. Where would the money come from?

I decided to stay in Los Angeles.

FLOATING THROUGH LIFE

Another reason I decided to stay put was because I never moved out when I started working full time at Ralphs after high school. Living with Mom was easy. Free rent. No utilities. Come and go as I pleased.

I liked my lifestyle during my early twenties. I usually worked nights, which meant that I was free during the day to do what I wanted: go to the beach, hang out with friends, and play basketball. Lots of afternoons I joined pick-up games at local parks, Valley College, or wherever basketball players congregated. City Leagues scheduled their games in the early evening, so I had time to play competitively and still be at work if I was working graveyard.

I tested my game by trying out and making a semi-pro team called Magnum Force, the name of the second film in the Clint Eastwood *Dirty Harry* series that was the rage in the 1970s. We played all over the Valley, some parts of Pasadena, and Eagle Rock as well as Los Angeles. Our team was stocked with college players who weren't quite good enough for the NBA and a few players who played a season or two in the pros. We didn't get paid anything, but we did receive a duffle bag, free shoes, and food vouchers. I didn't ride the pine, either; I got playing time and averaged eight points a game. I thrived on the upgrade in competition.

When I returned from Oregon, there was no grand game plan percolating in my mind. I picked up odd jobs until I sorted things out. Worked as a fire inspector for an insurance company. Did some secret shopping. Coached varsity basketball at North Hollywood High, where I was one of the assistants on the bench. I also gave college basketball one more shot.

In the fall of 1978, I enrolled at Pierce College, a community college in nearby Woodland Hills, and tried out for the basketball team. I was cut immediately. This time I was too *old*. Yup, at twenty-three years of age, I didn't mesh with a squad made up mostly of teenagers—eighteen- and nineteen-year-olds. The irony didn't escape me.

None of my part-time jobs paid particularly well or came with any benefits that I had enjoyed in the grocery industry. Suddenly, things like health insurance, paid vacation, time-and-a-half for overtime, and double time on holidays looked pretty good.

I decided to reach out to some of my old friends at Ralphs and ask if there were any job openings. I said all the right things about making a mistake, letting my emotions get the better of me, and look at all the life experiences I enjoyed in the interim. I was a better, more well-rounded person. Certainly more mature.

Sure, we got a place for you, Frankie.

This time, I was assigned to my neighborhood Ralphs—a super-market on Sherman Way and Woodman in Van Nuys. The job title was assistant grocery manager. I was starting all over again, at No. 6 on the management ladder, but I didn't mind. I had no commute and was out of central L.A., where crazy stuff happened. The Valley was a safer place to live. Everyone knew that.

One day—I was back to working daytime hours—a burly white guy in a big overcoat walked in. The fact that we were in the middle of a summer heat wave raised an eyebrow. Sorry, but when you spend all day watching people stroll around a supermarket, you get used to certain behavior. He wasn't in Ralphs to pick up a few things. Instead, he was getting the lay of the land.

After checking over his shoulder, he made a beeline for me. At this Ralphs, I was positioned at the main checkout stand, known as the "front desk," where the managers hung out.

"Hey," he said, grabbing my attention. Then he opened up his over-coat. Tucked inside was a double-barrel shotgun. "Open the safe," he commanded.

My heart rate shot up. I tried acting as nonchalantly as I could. "Okay. We're cool. I'll open up."

We had two safes at the front desk. One was a safe that I knew the combination to. I opened that one up in a jiffy—and showed him it was empty.

"What about the bottom one?" the robber asked.

"I don't have the combination."

Then I heard another voice say, "That's an easy way to lose your life."

I looked up to my left and saw a similarly dressed bandit pointing a pistol at me.

"Open the bottom safe," he demanded, waving the weapon at me.

I zoned in on this guy. "I'll give you anything you want," I said. "See, here's a money drop."

The empty safe had a chute that we used to "drop" money that was paper-clipped with a string attached to it so that we could retrieve the money if we had a run on cash.

I pulled on the string and produced a small stack of $100 and $20 bills. "See, there's money right there," I said.

"The bottom safe," he repeated.

"Can't open it. I don't know the combination, and it's time-locked. Listen, I'll give you everything in the store that's not time-locked."

What I said seemed to pacify the robbers. They were becoming aware that this heist was taking too long.

I didn't wait for them to decide what to do next. I opened the register at my checkstand and showed them the cash tray—and adroitly pressed a silent alarm.

The first robber stuffed a fistful of greenbacks into a plastic bag while the other kept his gun trained on me. Then they hit three or four registers. I kept expecting the police to bust through the entrance doors, guns drawn, just like in a cop show, but authorities never arrived. I would find out later that I had risked my life tripping the silent alarm for nothing.

The bandits escaped, and another robbery meant another round of police reports to fill out. Even though I had another exciting story to share in the break room, this time around I was sobered by the experience. I had heard too many stories through the grocery grapevine—stories that never ended well for the employee. I thought of the Du-pars employee shot during a robbery attempt. That could have been me.

When my boss asked me how I was doing, I was honest. Having a pistol pointed at me by someone who could have been crazy enough to shoot was too close for comfort.

"Okay, we'll find you someplace quieter," my boss said.

I was shipped off to the Ralphs in Glendale, which felt like I was being put out to pasture. This Ralphs was located in a quiet area near an old folk's home. Nobody was in that store. There was nothing to do. I felt like I was managing a retirement home.

After a year, I was so bored that I quit Ralphs a second time.

This was 1980. I was twenty-five years old, still trying to figure out life.

It was time to try something new.

10

MARY JANE

Trying something new meant moving out of my childhood home. It was about time I was on my own.

I picked a one-bedroom apartment in Burbank. My most important possession was my stereo system. I had a pair of JBL speakers that stood three feet high, two feet wide with base woofers the size of hubcaps. I would crank that music to levels that made the windows shake. When Zeppelin was on the turntable, it was like I was back at the Forum, lost in the noise and distortion coming out of Jimmy Page's Gibson guitar.

My neighbors didn't share the same appreciation for Page's virtuosity as I did. I had people knocking on my doors at all hours telling me to turn it down. The police came to my door on two occasions, saying they received complaints. It was like I had no filter, no consideration for anyone else. I was blown out in every way, shape, and form. That's how out of control I was. I was jacked to the nines.

One of the benefits of getting my own place was moving in closer proximity to my father and stepmother, who lived in Burbank a couple of miles from my apartment complex. Even though our relationship had always been complicated, that was another reason the move felt right.

The first time I visited Dad, he said there was something he wanted to show me in his backyard. Turned out, Dad had gone into horticulture. Everywhere I looked, there were six-foot high marijuana plants. It was like a forest back there. He certainly wasn't trying to hide anything from the neighbors.

"Anytime you want to get high, you can get high with me," he said. This was his way of saying, *I just want you to know that I smoke pot.*

I was surprised. I thought only people my age smoked dope. But Dad explained he got introduced to pot when he started working in Hollywood. Weed was the new thing in the late Sixties and prevalent on the set. He fell right in and smoked with the production crew. Actors, too.

When I visited Dad that day, I had never smoked pot. Not in high school, not while I worked at Ralphs. I was an athlete, a basketball player, remember? I was careful about what I put into my body, and that included alcohol. I rarely drank after what happened on my eighteenth birthday. Mom threw a party for me and packed our washing machine with beer and ice. A bunch of my friends came over, and we all got blitzed. I felt awful having the spins and throwing up. I swore I would never drink to excess again.

Even though I didn't leap at the chance to smoke dope with Dad, I appreciated the sentiment behind the gesture. This was his way of reaching out to me, father to son. "Thanks for the offer, Dad. Maybe I'll take you up on it some day," I said.

Not long after visiting Dad, I started dating a young woman named Sherry. She was into having fun and told me so. One evening, she came over to my place and suggested that we get high together before having sex. That seemed like a reasonable request at the time, so that's what we did. Too bad the timing of smoking my first joint didn't work out for Dad.

Procuring the drugs wasn't something I felt comfortable doing. As long as Sherry was the supplier, I was fine with lighting up a joint. Around the same time, I was hanging out with Bob, one of my best friends. We got to talking about various subject matters, and the topic turned to my newfound pot experiences. Hearing me tell about my experiences with Sherry prompted Bob to ask if I wanted to smoke weed some time.

"Sure," I replied.

"Here's what we'll do. I'll come over Saturday night with my stash. You provide the steaks and we'll have a party."

Since he was furnishing the weed, that sounded like a great plan.

The following weekend, Bob arrived at my apartment, a gallon-sized baggy stuffed with marijuana tucked in the crook of his right arm. To my inexperienced eyes, it looked like he had brought a sizeable amount of weed with him. We got down to business and smoked our first joint. Then I put the steaks inside the oven. We smoked some more. And some more.

Suddenly, my face started getting numb. The sensation felt really weird. I looked over at Bob sitting on my couch. His eyes got big, and then he keeled over and passed out. I panicked. Who should I call?

I knew just the person—my father. "Dad, get over here now. I'm in trouble, and if anything happens to me, know that I love you."

I wanted him to hear that last thought because I really thought I was gonna die. That's how weird I felt.

I was so out of it that I didn't notice the steaks burning to a crisp inside the oven. When Dad arrived, I managed to open the front door in my incapacitated state. Smoke from the oven and the pot session billowed out. It's amazing that we didn't set off any smoke alarms within a four-block radius.

"What did you get into?" he asked.

I showed him the drug paraphernalia and half-empty baggy.

"I can't believe you smoked that much," he said. Then again, he was an expert.

"You've got to lie down." Dad led me to my bedroom, then assisted me onto my bed. "Just sleep it off," he counseled.

I don't know when or how Bob left because I was out of it for three days. It took two months to get the pungent residue of pot smoke out of the apartment.

I don't have a real good memory of how long Sherry and I continued to date after that episode. She was just another girlfriend in a string of relationships during my twenties. After Sherry, I got to know a pretty young woman that I'll call Regina Lightfoot. A full-blooded Native American, she was dating one of my basketball buddies who used to come over to the house for pick-up games.

One day, he was bragging about cheating on her and how stupid she was for being none the wiser. I took offense to hearing him say that. Ray was the chauvinistic type who thought girls were put on this earth to be used by guys when they wanted and how they wanted. I didn't think he should treat Regina that way, so I told her what Ray had said.

"You're lying," she said. "Absolutely, Ray wouldn't say that."

Of course, Regina confronted Ray, who was blindsided. "Where did you hear that?" he asked her.

"Frank told me."

The next installment of this soap opera occurred when Ray found me in my driveway shooting baskets. He was ready to fight. "How dare you rat me out," he said as he circled me, ready to pounce.

I held up my hands. "Dude, you were cheating on her. That wasn't fair."

Ray stopped circling and let his arms drop. "Okay, I'll break up with her, and you can have her. She means nothing to me anyway."

Regina thought I was her knight in shining armor after that. When I asked her if she wanted to go out on a date, she readily accepted. We soon became lovers, and she was my steady girl for two years until we went our separate ways.

Next, I met another beautiful woman who worked in the bakery department at Ralphs La Brea. We were inseparable for a couple of years. After the relationship ended, I took up with another foxy woman I met at Ralph's.

In my own way, I was following my dad's advice. I remember him telling me after I graduated from high school, "Never get married. Sleep with as many women as you can." I took that advice to heart because it was the only advice I heard about having a relationship with the opposite sex.

For a fleeting moment, whenever I was in the loving arms of an attractive young woman, the hole in my heart was filled.

RACING FORM

After I left Ralphs a second time, my dad said he'd try to find work for me in the movie industry. Of course, when you work on the studio's schedule, that means a lot of waiting around for the phone to ring. It just so happened that things were slow. I'd ask Dad what the deal was, and he'd shrug his shoulders. *That's Hollywood for you.*

With little work and much time on my hands, I started visiting Santa Anita and Hollywood Park because I loved watching thoroughbred horses run. But there was a lot of waiting between races, so even that diversion got boring.

I started laying down some $2 bets to keep my mind in the game. I studied the handicap sheets that were hawked at the track and learned how to sift though *The Racing Form* for pertinent information on past performances of horse and jockey. I won a few times. Maybe I should rephrase that: I won more than I lost, which was enough to keep me coming back.

I fell into a routine: my life consisted of waking up in the morning, walking to the local liquor store, purchasing a *Racing Form*, going back to my apartment, studying for a couple of hours, and then going to the track for the afternoon to lay down a few bets on the nags.

My bets got bolder and bolder. I risked more and more money. But I kept coming out ahead at the end of the day—pocketing enough to pay the bills and support myself. I was starting to enjoy the lifestyle of a professional gambler. I felt like I was smarter than all the working stiffs in the world.

When you go to the racetrack every day, you get to know the regulars. We'd swap tips on the Daily Doubles and trade gossip on the jockeys. You could say gambling at the racetrack became an obsession right alongside basketball. I was consumed by horse racing.

Dad dropped by the apartment one morning. "I've got something important to tell you," he declared.

I gulped because I wasn't sure where this was going.

"I've got a safety deposit box in Universal City. If anything ever happens to me, I want you to go in there and clean it out. So I need to get you signed onto the account and a key."

Universal City was the home of Universal Studios, where Dad worked most of the time. We dropped by the Bank of America branch and got all the necessary paperwork done. Dad expressly said not to tell anyone about the existence of the safety deposit box.

I wondered what the secrecy was all about. And what was in the box?

After a few weeks, curiosity got the better of me. I showed up at the bank, signed the necessary form, and was led to the vault. After I received the long safety deposit box, I huddled in a corner for privacy and lifted the cover. The box contained only one item: cash—and lots of it. I counted $100s, $20s, and small bills. Total: right around $6,000.

Dad is stashing away a lot of money. I didn't know exactly where the pile of greenbacks came from, but I remembered my father talking one time about how he often received a per diem, in cash, while on the set, to pay for meals and incidentals. Wherever the money came from, this was his rainy day fund.

Back at the track, I hit a losing streak. The regulars told me that bad luck happens to everyone, but as I returned to my apartment with a lighter wallet each day, I had a sinking feeling in the pit of my stomach. The water line was rising quickly.

Then I remembered the gambler's dictum: You cut your losses by upping the ante. I searched the *Racing Form* for a horse that everyone overlooked. I've since forgotten his name, but let's call him Sure Bet. He was a 6-1 long shot, but in my mind, he was a can't miss for a variety of good reasons. I remember seeing Sure Bet in the paddock one time. His gleaming coat and broad chest took my breath away. His speed ratings checked out. His results were improving, right where they should be for a two-year-old.

The figure that popped in my mind was betting $500 on him—to win! A $3,000 payoff would more than make up for my losing streak and bankroll the rest of the season.

But $500 was a lot of money to risk on one race. If Sure Bet finished second or worse, I was out of the money.

Here was the rationale of a twenty-five-year-old rebellious, wounded guy who never really knew his father: *Dad owes me. He's going to invest in my gambling habit and see me through this streak of bad luck.*

I paid a visit to the safe deposit box. I removed $500, telling myself that I was just "borrowing" the money until I could return it after cashing in my winning ticket.

With me so far?

I couldn't wait to go out to the track and lay it all on the line for Sure Bet. It was all a matter of my luck turning around, and I was due.

I bet my $500 stake on this horse. I knew he was going to win. I took a seat in the grandstand and watched the horses being lead into the starting gate. The anticipation rose to a fever pitch.

And they're off!

Sure Bet, to my horror, stumbled out of the gate. Within seconds, he was way behind the field. He never recovered and limped home, dead last.

My $500—ah, Dad's $500—was gone in less than two minutes. Up in smoke. Nothing to show for it.

Now it wasn't a matter of making up for my losses. I had to win Dad's $500 back. I returned to the safety deposit box and lifted more cash. Every few days, though, it seemed like I needed a refill. My luck wasn't changing.

About a month after Sure Bet cratered at the starting gate, I received a phone call from Dad. He was livid and lit into me.

"Where's the money?" he demanded. He evidently had been at the

safety deposit box to make a deposit. Instead, he noticed that someone had been making withdrawals. We both knew it had to be me.

"I lost it at the track."

"You what?"

"Dad, there was this horse named Sure Bet—"

What I heard next was a string of expletives that emphasized how I was a worthless son. "You need to get your @#$% back to work and get a real job! I want nothing to do with you!" And then he hung up the phone.

I could see Dad's point. But the rationalizations for my behavior came around to this point: *Screw you, Dad. That money was mine because you were never there for me.*

As for getting a full-time job, my options were limited since I didn't have a college degree and knew only the world of supermarkets. Like a homing pigeon, I got a job with Lucky's, a smaller supermarket chain with stores in California. I didn't want any responsibility or chance of looking down a gun barrel, so I took a full-time job as a night crew stocker. I asked my boss if I could bring my humongous stereo to work, and he said fine. Six nights a week, I blasted heavy rock standards throughout the store while we restocked the shelves. (This Lucky's, which was on the corner of Victory Boulevard and Coldwater Canyon Avenue in Van Nuys, closed at 11 p.m. every night.)

When you do repetitive work like lifting cans out of boxes and stacking them just so on the shelves, you have a lot of time to think.

I realized that I had a gambling problem. That had to stop, and it did. I couldn't bet on the ponies any longer. I still went to the track every now and then. I loved watching the horses run. I couldn't gamble any longer.

My luck had run out.

A MOVE TO UPSCALE

After a year or two with Lucky's, I got sick of working nights and looked at my options. A colleague told me to check out Gelson's Markets, a regional supermarket chain with six stores operating in Southern California.

Ooh, Gelson's was high class. Catered to the upper echelon. Known for being a retailer of fine foods, specialty brands, and pricey imported items. Sushi. Gelato. Baguettes and brioche. The supermarkets themselves were upscale, and some offered valet parking.

In the spring of 1982, I was hired at Gelson's Century City, the neighborhood of millionaires and movie stars. I was happy being hired on as a clerk. I didn't want to do management, and I didn't want to work nights. I just wanted to stock a shelf, run a register, flirt with the movie stars, and kibitz with the celebrities.

One time, actor Gregory Peck came in and asked me to help him find light bulbs.

"Why sure, Mr. Peck. If you'll follow me."

I led this Oscar-winning actor to the right aisle, and then he asked me whether he should get 75 watt light bulbs or 60 watt bulbs.

"Well, it all depends on how much light you're looking for," I said, which started a friendly ten-minute discussion. He was the sweetest guy, and his friendliness to an hourly employee like me left a lasting impression.

It was at Gelson's that I tried cocaine for the first time with some of the other clerks. No particular reason why; just something to do. One day I was so high that when the "beautiful people" and rich folks passed through my checkstand, I was more interested in chatting them up and becoming their friends than in ringing their items properly. (This was just before the changeover to scanner technology. We had to manually punch in the price totals.) I'm sure I gave away hundreds of dollars hitting the wrong keys because of my drug-addled brain.

I experimented a couple of more times with coke. I must have been high on something when, after a year at Gelson's, I had a blow-out with one of the managers. Once again, I followed an impulse and quit on the spot.

The next day, I received a phone call from the vice president of Gelson's, a guy named Don Lee. He was a big basketball fan and huge UCLA supporter. He knew about me as a basketball player, having been tipped off by a former Bruin player. He also knew I had joined the Gelson's team that played in a city league.

Mr. Lee got right to the point. "Frank, we don't want to lose you. Let's move you to Gelson's in North Hollywood."

"Fine," I said. "Just get me away from that idiot manager of yours."

It was at the Gelson's in North Hollywood, where a friend at work, Gary Stiles, introduced me to motorbikes and arranged the purchase of my Honda FT500. Shortly after getting my motorbike in the spring of 1984, my sister, Theresa, asked me if I wanted to give her husband a hand with his airplane parts business. Rich Benjamin had a warehouse near the Van Nuys Airport that was filled with spare parts shipped from aircraft "boneyards" around the country as well as military installations. Think of a Pep Boys on steroids for private pilots.

Theresa said Rich could use some help organizing his parts inventory. That sounded like a nice change from stocking shelves, so I left Gelson's. Rich's company purchased crates of used airplane parts in lots, which needed to be catalogued. My job was to open up the crates, pull out the various parts, get rid of the grime, and note as much information as I could on a record-keeping form.

The work was as nasty as they come. I remember one time when a shipment of parts from an F-86 Sabre jet arrived at the warehouse. I had no idea who'd be interested in spare parts from a fighter jet that had its heyday during the Korean War, but that wasn't my worry.

Creepy creatures had lived and died in those crates, many of which hadn't been opened in thirty years. I spent half my time removing carcasses and dead bugs; the other half was wiping decades-old grease and oil from machined parts.

I was riding my motorcycle a lot because my car was so unreliable—and because I liked to ride. The secondhand Chevy Caprice that I purchased from Rich's father for $1,500 came with generous financing terms: $100 a month and no interest.

I needed a car for transporting groceries and the infrequent times it rained in Southern California. The problem was that I could never be certain if the junker would start up each time I turned the ignition.

Like the time I was a secret shopper at a Glendale Savings Bank in Glendora.

11

GO YOUR OWN WAY

After my motorcycle accident on the 101 freeway, the plan was to give myself at least six months in Lake Tahoe to sift through where I wanted to go in life and search for answers to why I survived.

Late one night, the phone rang in the cabin. My roommate, Morgan Christopher, was on the line, sounding like he was in dire straits.

"You gotta help me," he said.

"Hold on, Morgan. Where are you?"

"Placer County Sheriff's Station."

The source of his phone call was surprising—but not unexpected. Life had been a downward spiral for Morgan ever since he had to shutter his pizza restaurant; there hadn't been enough business to keep the doors open. Morgan had debts and hadn't found work elsewhere. He'd been staying out late a lot of nights.

"What happened?"

"Well, it's like this. I got stopped after leaving a party." Morgan explained that he had been drinking and driving, so he was arrested and tossed in the county slammer.

"Can you bail me out?" he asked.

"What about bailing yourself out?" I rejoined.

"I don't have any money."

"And I do?"

I had just enough money to pay for three more months in Tahoe. That was the rest of my life savings. But I couldn't turn my back on Morgan. He'd been a lifelong friend.

"How much do you need?"

"A thousand bucks."

That would tap me out. But my chum needed a get-out-of-jail card.

"I have to wait until morning to go to the bank," I said.

"Just hurry," Morgan said.

First thing in the morning, I borrowed a truck and emptied my bank account. Then I drove the cash over to the county lock-up and posted bail. Now what was I going to do?

I took stock. Three months in Tahoe had seemed like three years. I'll admit that I had a hard time with the transition from sunny Southern California to a four-season winter wonderland where it was freezing cold outside. Another snowstorm had recently passed through, and piles of snow were banked high around Sunnyside.

Emotionally, I had gone through a lot since arriving in Tahoe. There were numerous flashbacks, which spooked me. I remember going down to the lake, where I'd look across the water and hear screams coming out of the deep blue water. That really freaked me out. I told Morgan about the screams and asked him if I was hearing dead people or victims who drowned. He didn't have an answer for me.

Then I wondered if what materialized on the lakeshore was a metaphysical response to everything that had occurred since June 17. Maybe I was a fish out of water in Lake Tahoe and needed to pull the plug on this diversion from real life.

I called my father. We were working on patching things up after my hand was caught in the bank vault cookie jar. We hadn't bridged the gap totally, but we were talking. Dad had taken a big step toward reconciliation when he wrote me a long letter shortly after I arrived in Tahoe. He told me that he was proud of what I was doing—taking a sabbatical from life to rethink and recharge. The tone of the entire letter was loving and supportive.

Wow, Dad wrote that?

When I reached out to my father this time, I told him, "Dad, I want to come back to L.A. I need to get some work. I'm out of money."

At first, Dad resisted. "You belong in Tahoe," he said. "You've made this step, a great step. You should stay up there."

I explained the situation with Morgan and how my money was gone.

There weren't any jobs in the middle of winter. "It's time," I said. "I need to earn some money."

"Okay, I'll work ya," he said. Those were sweet-sounding words. Dad was president of his lighting union, well-established in the movie industry as a lighting director. He'd told me stories about working with Elvis Presley and how more than a few people had asked him if he and Elvis were brothers because they shared a resemblance. Dad was one of those very good-looking guys who was popular on the set. Movie stars like James Garner and Telly Salvalas loved Dad when they were filming *The Rockford Files* and *Kojak*. With his connections, he could surely get me work on a movie or a commercial, doing something useful and earning a paycheck.

Dad drove up to the cabin in Tahoe, and I threw my belongings in the back of his truck. Then we drove back to L.A. together. It would turn out to be an up-and-back trip for Dad, nineteen hours straight on the road.

On the drive south, he offered me a joint. I didn't see how I could turn him down.

Call it father-son bonding time.

GETTING SETTLED

I moved in with Dad and Anita upon my return from Tahoe—but only because I had nowhere else to go. Mom had sold the old place and had moved into a small, one-bedroom apartment, so I didn't want to couch-surf with her.

Dad wasn't thrilled to have a twenty-nine-year-old son under his roof. I vowed to get a place of my own as soon as I had enough money to cover first and last month rent and a security deposit.

True to his word, Dad got me a job on a couple of Ford commercials, which replenished my coffers. Morgan also reimbursed me for posting bail, which helped me move into another apartment in Burbank.

A year after the motorcycle crash, there was a legal settlement. I received a $6,000 check for pain and suffering. My lawyer really wanted me to trump up my injuries, but I was happy to be alive and wanted to put the past behind me. I had survived a bone-jarring crash when I shouldn't have. I didn't want to be one of those scammers who pretended to be injured the rest of his life.

Heather received $100,000, which covered her medical bills and not much more. The driver got off with a speeding ticket. No jail time, even though they found drugs in the car.

Time to move on. While I was figuratively starting all over, I didn't want to go back to the grocery business. With a small cushion of money, I bought a slow-poke '65 VW Beetle for $500 and devoted myself to getting back into shape. I joined a gym in Canoga Park called the Left Hook, where I trained as a boxer. The owner trained actor Sylvester Stallone for his *Rocky* movies, so I studied the sweet science for three or four days a week under his practiced eye. It felt good working up a serious sweat and getting out my aggression by working the speed bag and punching bag. Across the street from the Left Hook was my physical therapist, who continued to work on the kinks in my back.

Besides working out and doing odd jobs, I read a lot, continuing the quest I started in Lake Tahoe. I hadn't yet put the pieces together on how I got hit and stayed alive, but I figured that some type of revelation would come some day.

One Sunday afternoon, I had an urge to revisit the crash scene— right at 6 p.m., the official time of the massive collision that had changed my life. I drove along Burbank Boulevard, a frontage road, and got on the Ventura Freeway at Hayvenhurst Avenue in Encino. Then I headed in a westerly direction on the 101.

As the four-lane freeway approached Balboa Boulevard, I spotted a gap between Lane 4 and the off-ramp, set off by a long triangle of white striping. I slowed down and drove my VW bug into the gap, then stopped the car. Being parked between the freeway and the off ramp carried a bit of danger since a steady stream of fast-moving cars and trucks sped by my window, but I had to stop there. This was holy ground; the spot where I got run down on the Ventura Freeway.

I came to a halt because I was hungry to find truth. I was still searching for answers to the Big Questions:

- Why did I survive a smackdown by a runaway Corvette?
- What's life all about anyway?
- Who are we, and why are we here?

Memories came flooding back. I remembered getting up from the freeway, and the first thing I saw was a tree next to the freeway. It was like I had never really looked at a tree before or thought about what a tree does.

There was no reason why I should have walked away from an up-close-and-personal encounter with the front grill of a speeding sports car going 110 mph. The Corvette should have splattered my flesh and bones everywhere. How come my skull wasn't cracked in two with brain matter flowing onto the concrete? I hadn't been wearing a helmet.

My late Sunday afternoon drive-by on the Ventura Freeway became a weekly ritual that would last for many years.

THE QUEST CONTINUES

My quest for answers took me back to talk show host Michael Benner on KLOS on Sunday nights, starting at midnight. His *Impact* program explored spirituality in a compelling way that appealed to my sensibilities. When Michael described how focus brought to bear the power of the conscious mind and how passion brought to bear the power of the subconscious mind, I felt he was speaking right to my heart. He finished that thought by describing how the conscious and unconscious minds can come together in harmony, which allows something magical to happen: the creation of a third mind, or higher consciousness.

Oh, how I wanted higher consciousness. This would be where my search for answers would reach fruition. I learned from Michael that when thoughts and feelings came into my consciousness, it was up to me to choose to empower the positive ones and release the negative ones. In other words, I had to release the horrible memories of the motorcycle accident. If I did this, I could discover happiness since happiness came from my thoughts and what I thought about.

I began practicing practical steps I could take to reach a higher level of consciousness. I started with closing my eyes and slowing down my mind. I cut out distractions.

Then I took a deep breath and imagined that I was in a very safe and peaceful place. This was a place where I could be set free from the parameters of the world yet tangible enough that I could see this place and hear the surrounding sounds. This was a place I could reach through meditation, introspection, reflection, and prayer.

Every Sunday night, like a devoted acolyte, I turned to 95.5 FM to hear from my learned teacher. I felt like Michael Benner was speaking directly to *me* because there's an intimacy in radio, a one-to-one connection that no other medium can match. Radio reaches people through just one of the five senses—hearing—but this is to the medium's benefit, not detriment. The sound of Michael's soothing words, which were richly phrased and imaginatively used, created a picture in my mind. This "theater of the mind" touched me in a deeper way than any film or television show could ever expect to do.

Michael's thoughtful diction and erudite insights captured my attention from the opening minutes of each show. Any time he announced that he would be lecturing in person, I was in the audience to soak up his ageless wisdom. I always stuck around when he was done to say hello or ask follow-up questions. I believe he sensed he had a true believer on his hands. I'd characterize our budding relationship as cordial, but friendly.

One Sunday night in the spring of 1985, Michael announced during his show that he was looking for an intern. My ears perked up. Interning with Michael Benner would deepen the teacher-student bond between us. He also mentioned on his program that he would be lecturing the following Tuesday night, so I made sure I was in attendance. I approached him when he was finished with his remarks.

"I hear you're looking for an intern. That's something I'd be interested in," I said.

"That's great to hear, Frank, but you'll need to apply like everyone else. Write me a letter explaining why you're applying and what you hope to gain from the experience."

I asked Michael to tell me more about the position, and he replied that his intern would give him a hand on Tuesday mornings with his correspondence, running errands, filing tapes—that sort of thing. Maybe five or six hours a week.

I sat down at my dining room table and wrote that I viewed him as a leader and a teacher who knew a great deal about the human condition. "Being around you will give me an opportunity to benefit from your life experiences," I noted.

A few days later, he phoned me to let me know I got the job. I was thrilled; I wouldn't be paid anything, but I didn't care. This was a chance to hang out with someone I looked up to.

Every Tuesday morning, I drove over to Michael's house in Granada Hills in the Valley and helped him work through his backlog of mail and whatever else needed to be done. He knew my motorcycle crash story, so after a month together, he asked me if I wanted to go on a bike trip to the Grand Canyon and back. "I've got two Suzuki 850s in the garage. Would you be up for it?" he asked.

As far as I was concerned, if I never sat on the leather seat attached to a motorcycle again, I'd die a happy man, but I didn't see how I could say no. I'm glad we did our version of *Easy Rider*, a pair of free-spirited wayfarers traversing hundreds of miles of lonely desert between L.A and the Grand Canyon. The way I looked at things, this was another chance to hang out with a well-read intellectual who could expound on anything metaphysical—air, earth, fire, and water—with great insight and authority.

Michael loved to teach, and I loved to listen. When he invited me to watch him do his show for a few hours on Sunday night, I could barely contain my excitement.

I remember the first time I walked into the sprawling, 45,000-square-foot broadcast facility that occupied ten acres off of La Cienega in Culver City near downtown. This was the home of KABC, one of the oldest radio stations in the United States that dated back to 1925. Sister station KLOS, found on 95.5 FM, debuted in 1969 with its rock music format.

After we moved to Southern California, I grew up listening to Vin Scully's melliferous voice broadcasting Dodgers baseball on KABC, 790 on the dial. During my junior high years at bedtime, I tuned in to Vinnie on a pocket-sized transistor radio tucked under my pillow.

When I was led to Michael's soundproof studio and saw all the microphones, sound boards, carts, and record albums for the first time, it was love at first sight, almost like I heard the pealing of bells and a choir singing. The idea of sitting behind a microphone and talking to potentially tens of thousands, even hundreds of thousands of people, all over Southern California seemed powerful and magical.

The experience of watching a live radio show enthralled me. I didn't want to leave, even after Michael signed off at 5 a.m. Two days later when I arrived at his house to help him with his correspondence, I told him I knew what I wanted to do with my life.

"What's that?" Michael asked.

"I want to get into radio."

12

WE ARE THE WORLD

One Sunday night, I hung out at KLOS and watched Michael Benner from the control booth. I sat next to his call screener, Jim Nelson, and observed how Jim talked to listeners who phoned in and wanted to ask Michael a question or describe a spiritual experience they had.

With a talk-show format, the quality of Michael's broadcast relied heavily on whether the callers had anything worthwhile to say or something interesting to add to the topic of spirituality or anything else on their minds. Jim was a gatekeeper whose role was to determine, on the fly and by the seat of his pants, whether the caller would enhance the listening experience.

"Here's what you're looking for," he told me during a commercial break. "On a stereotypical AM station, you call in and they ask, 'What's your name and where are you calling from?' Next thing you know, you're on the air. We do things differently here. We screen calls much more extensively. You want to make sure people are well-spoken, thoughtful, and lucid, especially at this time of night. You want them to have something clear and concise to share or a specific question they want answered. The last thing we want is for them to get on the air and ramble—or not saying anything at all. Dead air is an anathema to good radio."

From my vantage point, I thought Jim had a really interesting job. Being the guy who determined which callers got on the air got me thinking how cool this would be to do some day.

One Tuesday morning when I was at Michael's house, I mentioned that if the opportunity ever presented itself, I'd like to become his call screener.

Michael grunted. "Won't happen. Jim has been working with me for three years and really loves what he does."

"Well, keep me in mind. I really want to be your screener if the opportunity presents itself."

Michael didn't respond, but I had listened to him say that when you give voice to an objective—"declare" that you want something to occur—then the power of the universe within you would make that happen.

Two weeks later, Jim Nelson was handed his pink slip. I don't remember why he got fired or what circumstances brought about his dismissal, but the screener position was open. As soon as I heard the jolting news, I phoned Michael and reminded him of our conversation.

"I can't just give the job to you," he responded. "You'll have to apply just like everyone else."

This time, though, I was applying with KLOS, not Michael Benner. I hustled over to Culver City and filled out a job application, writing on every line to build an open-and-shut case as to why I would make a great screener for *Impact*.

I was brought in for an interview, and my passion showed through. Two weeks later, I had the job, which was a part-time position. But at least I had one big foot in the control booth. My first Sunday in the screener's chair was September 22, 1985.

KLOS actually hired me as the program coordinator for *two* broadcasts: Michael Benner's *Impact* show on Sunday nights and another show on spirituality that aired earlier on Sunday morning from 4-7 a.m. Pay was $180 for a *very* long day that began at 3 a.m. Sunday and lasted until dawn on Monday morning.

A young woman named Gayl Murphy was the host of the early Sunday morning show, the title of which escapes me. She worshipped Michael Benner. Thought he hung the moon. The first thing she did when she arrived was spread crystals on the soundboard for "energy." She said in the metaphysical world of gemstones, crystals could help us in physical, emotional, and spiritual ways. Because all gemstones come from Mother Earth, she said, each one was naturally fully charged with powerful energies.

Whatever.

I didn't swallow her spiel, but I kept my thoughts to myself. As for Michael, he had some mojo. He was a deep thinker. Cerebral and thoughtful. He was always talking about reaching your potential, looking at ways to improve yourself, and the power of positive thinking. He told a story on the air one time about a French psychologist and hypnotherapist from the early 1900s named Émile Coué who urged people to command their own reality and "brainwash" their thoughts to think a certain way. His mantra spoke to the power of positivity: *If you think it, therefore it will be.* Just like how I thought I would become Michael's screener.

Émile Coué also had another expression: "Every day, in every way, I'm getting better and better." When people would call in and ask Michael how he was doing, he would invariably say, "Better and better." He was always accentuating the affirmative.

Sitting behind the glass partition and screening Michael's calls was as interesting a job as I thought it would be. The first thing I listened for from the caller was clarity of speech. Did he or she speak clearly and in complete sentences, or did the caller chop off word endings and slur syllables?

Let's face it: when you hosted a show on a rock station that didn't begin until midnight and ran into the wee hours, you were going to get callers who may have been smoking dope or under the influence. If I suspected someone was stoned or tipsy, I'd let them down easy. "I'm afraid you're not focused on the topic tonight," I said soothingly. "Listen to the show some more, and then you're welcome to call back next week."

The screening process took several minutes, sometimes longer, but it was all about due diligence. The best calls came from those who said they were searching for the meaning of life. I put them to the front of the queue because that was a "perennial" right in Michael's wheelhouse. He would patiently listen to their story, draw them out with the right questions, and then riff on the importance of a holistic spirituality without borders or confining dogmas—or wherever his brilliant mind took him. With pitch-perfect intonation, he'd talk about how our minds, bodies, and spirits can embark on a sacred journey to discover life's meaning.

A typical exchange would go like this:

Caller: Michael, I heard you talking about how much power we can have as individuals. I would really like more of that in my life. What are some ways I can tap into that power?

Michael: The power starts from within because the power of human potential cannot be denied. Many individuals do not give themselves permission to tap into a grand inner vision that fuels their inspiration and drives them to change the course of their lives. I want you to release to the world your profound mission in life. Let your inner talents emerge. All your unique and visionary ways will flourish if you do. Once you unlock your human potential, you will see brightness where others see darkness. Are you willing to empower yourself and receive clarity on the source of power within?

I loved what Michael had to say. Everything made sense! He was showing me a path to self-development and fulfillment that began when I started my quest to find truth. Michael was right: motorcycle crashes *were* transformational. Because of what happened on the 101, I was open to a body of spiritual teaching that Michael described as "ageless wisdom." Who better than my holy host to guide me through a systematic and comprehensive account of the evolution of consciousness in man and nature? I counted myself fortunate to be in the presence of a learned teacher who effortlessly shared fascinating insights into the human condition.

For the next couple of years as his call screener, I learned a lot more about ageless wisdom from Michael, augmented my understanding by reading books from noted spirituality authors like Alice Bailey and Benjamin Creme, and participated in Whole Life Expos where like-minded people gathered in the Southland. Because I wanted to devote plenty of free time to explore these avenues to self-improvement—in other words, not work a full-time job—I lived a frugal lifestyle by keeping my expenses to a minimum and not taking on debt.

Thanks goodness my sound system and VW Bug were paid for. What more did a guy in his early thirties need? Food wasn't important to me. I didn't cook, so I ate a lot of Top Ramen, canned soups, and taco shop burritos. I rented a bedroom in a four-bedroom house in Tarzana for $400 a month, which was cheap digs, especially for a horse property where I was able to gaze upon stallions and mares roaming around a fenced enclosure.

My love for horses hadn't changed, even if I had lost a lot of my money—and my Dad's—at the horse track.

GETTING CLOSER

As Michael and I grew closer, I found out that he liked to smoke marijuana. He said the dried flowers and subtending leaves and stems of the female cannabis plant put him into a reflective state to consider the questions of the universe.

Hearing him speak appreciatively of grass gave me an idea: Wouldn't that be great if Michael and my father lit up together? I organized a Saturday night at Dad's place in Burbank. When we arrived, Dad showed off his pot plants to Michael, who was suitably impressed. Anita prepared a nice meal, and then we got loaded to the point where Michael passed out at the table.

I further ingratiated myself to the host of *Impact* when I volunteered to become his audio guy at his public lectures. I brought in the equipment to record his talks, which I put on audiocassette tapes that were popular in the 1980s. When Michael was finished, I sat at the back table and collected money from folks buying cassettes of his past lectures. I began to be identified with Michael as his assistant. I was his screener, his recording guy, and his roadie.

During the summer of 1987, Michael notified our program director that he'd be gone the weekend of August 16-17. He'd been asked to emcee a Harmonic Convergence event somewhere.

We were both jazzed about the upcoming Harmonic Convergence, which was receiving a lot of attention in the media. Perhaps you remember the Harmonic Convergence, if you are a certain age. If you're too young, let me give you a primer.

The Harmonic Convergence was a supernatural phenomenon that supposedly happened once every 10,000 years. And wouldn't you know it, the Harmonic Convergence was set to occur the weekend of August 16-17 when the planets in our solar system would align in an unusual configuration that would greatly amplify their spiritual energy. This supernatural event would cause the two spirit portals in the North and South Poles to overlap and envelop the physical world with a purple aura.

Those promoting the Harmonic Convergence promised that there was going to be a great shift in the earth's energy from warlike to peaceful. Everyone would follow his or her bliss after the Harmonic Convergence passed. At least, that was the hype in the weeks before the weekend of August 16-17.

When I heard Michael was going away for a Harmonic Convergence appearance, I knew we needed a replacement host. As I bandied names around my head, I realized that this was a golden opportunity for *me* to sit in his chair. I could be the host of *Impact*. I could try my hand at live radio.

"What do you think?" I asked Michael. "Can I fill in for you?"

Michael had no objections. "Check with the boss," he said.

I sought out the program director. He saw no reason not to let me guest host. "But you'll have to join the union," he said.

KLOS was a union shop. The union the PD was referring to was AFTRA—the American Federation of Television and Radio Artists. To me, this news was just a bump in the road. How hard could that be to fill out a form and join a union? "Sure, I can do that," I said, eager to please.

"It's not cheap," he said.

"How much?"

"Fifteen hundred bucks," the program director said. "Look, it's crazy for you to fill in for Michael one time and make a few hundred dollars, but if that's what you want to do, I'll let you take *Impact* for the night."

I didn't hesitate. I really wanted to be the person behind the mic, not the glass partition. "I'm joining the union."

So that's what I did. AFTRA was real good about letting me make a small down payment and working out a payment plan.

I filled in on the Sunday night, and there was plenty to talk about. The Harmonic Convergence had fourteen "power points" throughout the world where hundreds of thousands celebrated a feeling of togetherness centered around the new vibrational frequencies coming out at the time. Places like Mount Shasta, California; Sedona, Arizona; Central Park in New York City; the Black Hills of South Dakota; Stonehenge, England; Mount Olympus in Greece; the Great Pyramids in Egypt; the Ganges River in India; and Mount Fuji in Japan hosted huge gatherings. Speakers said the Harmonic Convergence was the start of a time of cleansing that would last at least until 1992, preparing the Earth for contact with alien beings in 2012.

The year 2012 sure sounded like a long time in the future, and it was—twenty-five years. But I was more focused on the present, which was being the guest host on *Impact* and speaking into a microphone that transmitted my spoken thoughts into the ether for potentially millions to hear.

I absolutely loved the gig as radio host. Couldn't wait to do it again. Even better, the listening audience loved me, as evidenced by the sack of complimentary mail the station received after my first time on the air. I couldn't wait for Michael to go out of town again.

Little did either of us know that I would take Michael's job within three months.

A REGULATION MOVE

Just as the airline industry was deregulated in 1978, so was the radio industry in 1987 during the Reagan Administration. I didn't understand the particulars, but what I discovered was that Michael Benner's day job as the afternoon newsreader and traffic reporter for KLOS was "impacted" by deregulation. When management had to make cutbacks in the news room three months after my stint as guest host, it was like a game of musical chairs. When the music stopped, Michael was the last person standing—and out of a job with KLOS.

This time I didn't have to apply for Michael's job. The program director knew I was licking my chops. When he offered me the Sunday night show, I pumped the air with my fist. This was my big break.

To this day, I haven't forgotten what it was like sitting in Michael's chair on the Sunday after Thanksgiving, November 28, 1987, waiting for the red ON THE AIR light to light up my console. My mouth was dry, and my armpits were sweaty. What I soon found out right out of the gate, however, was that replacing someone who'd hosted the show for *ten years* wasn't going to be easy.

Michael's fans didn't mind me filling in when their guy was off for the week. They *did* mind that he was gone permanently. During the first few months, I got a lot of on-the-air callers asking questions like:

"Where's Michael?"

"When did Michael leave?"

"You're not Michael."

I understood their reaction. Michael Benner had owned the midnight to 5 a.m. airtime on Sunday nights. His Arbitron ratings put him at No. 1 for his time slot. He had a massive following. And now his old screener was warming his chair. A poser with little or next-to-no radio experience. People were expecting the rich voice and spiritual insights of Michael Benner; instead, they were stuck with me.

I got rained on pretty good. Being called Michael's "lackey assistant" was about the nicest thing people said. I don't know if I would have weathered the storm if there had been Twitter or Facebook in those days. Social media would have destroyed me.

Thank goodness I held my own in the ratings, so much so that when management decided to give Sunday morning talk show Gayl Murphy her pink slip, they asked me to take on her show as well.

In 1988, I started broadcasting Sunday morning from 4 a.m. to 7 a.m., and returned that night to do *Impact* from midnight until 5 a.m. Despite the ungodly hours, I loved it. I couldn't get enough.

Talking about spirituality, following my muse, giving voice to the big thoughts waiting to bust out of my brain, and being treated with respect by colleagues and co-workers because of the program I represented—all these reasons led me to believe that I had finally found my way. The way I did things, if callers wanted to talk about politics or the environment, I let them. Generally speaking, we were on the same left-of-center wavelength anyway. I mixed in a few songs as a change of pace.

The "Where's Michael?" questions abated when my first anniversary rolled around, which I was glad to see. But there was another type of caller that I grew to loathe—Christians who wanted to talk to me about Jesus or cite Scripture on the air. My tolerance for allowing them on the air was at hair-trigger levels:

> **Caller:** Frank, I've been listening to you for several weeks now, and all you talk about is how God is within all of us and just waiting to be unleashed in our lives if we meditate on that. Have you considered the claims of Christ, who said He is the one, true God? In John 14:6, Jesus says, "I am the way, the truth, and the life, no man cometh unto—"

> **Me:** Sir, this isn't a religious show. I know we discuss spirituality a great deal, but if I allowed you to preach from your book, anybody could call in with their book

and preach, and that's not what we're trying to do here.
Just to be clear. Any of you Christians out there who call
in to quote the Bible, don't waste your time. Next caller.

I wanted nothing to do with Christianity. I couldn't get those Jesus
Freaks off my show fast enough. I reminded listeners that I didn't talk
about two things: religion and sports.

Yet if someone called in and described himself as a Buddhist or
Hindu, the door was wide open. I'd speak deferentially about their quest
to find God. If the same person mentioned "His Holiness"—the Dalai
Lama, not Pope John Paul II—he had the floor. The same went for anyone identifying himself with Taoism, Western Occultism, or Far Eastern
mysticism. In my mind, those weren't religions. The disciplines of yoga
and meditation were worthy of respect as well.

Jesus Christ wasn't accorded the same deference. This apostate to
the Catholic faith wanted nothing to do with the person who hung on a
scary-looking cross.

FAMILY WAY

Something else happened in 1987: I got a young woman pregnant.

Her name was Karen, and she got pregnant the first night we slept
together. Some people have all the luck.

She was raised Catholic, like me. I guess there was a residue of good
old-fashioned Catholic guilt residing within our black souls. Karen told
me she wanted to keep the baby. I didn't have the heart to bring up other
options.

In fact, I went a step further. I felt like I should do the right thing and
marry Karen so I could be a father to the child. She agreed to marry me
and said her best friend was a minister. We had a little ceremony in her
backyard to make things official before Lindsay Marie Sontag arrived
on February 16, 1988. I tried to be there for my infant daughter, but our
relationship was a disaster waiting to happen.

Even though Karen and I lived together as a married couple, our
relationship was a catastrophe. After eighteen months under the same
roof, I couldn't take it anymore and moved out. But six months later, I
felt badly for Lindsay and decided to come back. Our marriage was still
as rocky as the shoals along Southern California beaches.

On my own volition, I sought counseling with a marriage and family counselor. After a couple of sessions, it was apparent that the marriage was never going to work. At our last meeting, the counselor imparted some final advice.

"Whatever you do, Frank," the counselor said, "stay in the house until Lindsay is at least four. They formulate so much in those early years, so be around her."

I followed that advice. I stayed in the home until Lindsay was four-and-a-half or so. But then the pressure and conflict got to me. I couldn't take it anymore, so I left again, and our union was dissolved.

I continued to stay in touch with Karen because I wanted to be a father to Lindsay, even though it was on a part-time basis. I'd take her on afternoon outings or grab a bite to eat with her. Her mother and I had things generally smoothed out—until the Northridge Earthquake toppled freeway overpasses and crumpled apartment buildings in the San Fernando area in early 1994. Karen was pretty shook up by the experience, but she wasn't alone. The 6.7 earthquake rattled a lot of nerves and caused billions of dollars of damage.

Karen decided she had to get out the Valley. She moved to Las Vegas, taking Lindsay with her. After a couple of years in the desert, she married someone she met in Vegas.

We both felt it was important that I stay in touch with my beautiful daughter. As soon as Lindsay was old enough to fly as an unaccompanied minor, Karen and I shuttled her back and forth on nonstop flights from Burbank to Las Vegas. She'd stay with me for a long weekend or a couple of weeks in summer, and then I'd put her back on the plane. Each good-bye was really hard to do.

ROCK 'N' ROLL JOCK

After a couple of years at KLOS, my program director asked me to drop by his office. He had a question for me: "Have you ever DJ'd?"

"Absolutely," I replied without hesitation. "In college."

I don't think Valley College even had a radio station, but it didn't matter. I lied through my teeth because I sensed he might ask me to fill in for well-known jocks like Jim Ladd or "Uncle Joe" Benson, just like I had for Michael Benner.

"We've got a couple of openings on Friday and Saturday nights, the midnight shifts," the PD said. "Interested in taking them on?"

Would I? And that's how I ended up jocking on Friday nights and

Saturday nights. The Saturday night show led right into my talk show from 4-7 a.m. on Sunday mornings, but everyone was cool with that. Then our news guy, Chuck Moshantz, said I could earn some extra cash by prerecording American news stories that were fed to nine different radio stations in Australia. I'd knock those out on Saturday mornings, usually after I took a ninety-minute nap on a futon in an empty office.

Then a classic rock station in Ventura, KZTR 96 FM, asked me if I wanted to fill in on their midnight-to-dawn graveyard shift. They liked my work well enough to offer me a regular Monday-through-Friday gig from 6 p.m. to 11 p.m. and Saturdays from noon to 6 p.m. I loved all that jocking, even though Fridays got pretty crazy. I'd jock until 11 p.m. at 96ZTR on Friday nights, then jump in my car and hustle to the KLOS studios in Culver City with minutes to spare. I'd do the midnight to 6 a.m. show, take a nap, and record news stories for Australian radio. Then I'd take another nap on the futon before driving *back* to Ventura for another six-hour stint playing classic rock hits on Saturday afternoon.

Working at KTZR added only $200 a week to my KLOS paycheck, but jocking six days a week, sometimes for as many as twelve hours a day, is where I gained my radio chops. It was all about ramping up the on-air experience.

Fortunately, I didn't have to choose the songs; both stations had music directors who determined the play lists. The days of DJs playing whatever they felt like ended in the '60s and '70s when popular music fragmented into smaller segments: pop music, R&B, classic rock, heavy metal, punk, country, and oldies. Program directors realized they had to target their music to reach certain audiences. They had their music directors put together carefully researched song lists, which were printed out for the DJ to play. I was told to work my way down the song list and play the songs in order. Never waver.

I'd been at KLOS for a couple of months when one night at 3 a.m., I decided to see if my boss was listening. I broke format and played "One More Look at You" by Barbara Streisand. The seven-minute song was a syrupy ballad from the 1976 movie, *A Star Is Born*, and was similar to "The Way We Were." I was taking a real chance.

My hot line never rang.

As far as I was concerned, that was my green light to break format in the future. Something told me that reaching into the Barbara Streisand discography one more time would be foolhardy, so I leaned more in the direction of *my* personal taste in music, which was heavy metal. Every now and then, when it was darkest before dawn, I slipped in songs like "Lovedrive" by the Scorpions, a West German heavy metal band (this was obviously before the Berlin Wall fell in 1989) and "High and Dry" from Def Leppard.

I didn't mind working seven days a week. I loved every minute jocking and being a talk-show host. I was finally doing something with my life. But it was engaging callers on *Impact* that really turned my jets. That's what kept me going the rest of the week.

As far as I was concerned, I was an evangelist—a proselytizer for the New Age.

13

DUST IN THE WIND

I liked being on the front lines of a broad-ranging, consciousness-raising movement as the host of *Impact*. A five-hour weekly talk show in the nation's second biggest city was quite a soapbox to stand on. Sure, the radio program came on at a time when most people were asleep. But if you've ever driven on L.A.'s freeways in the middle of the night, then the crowded lanes and sea of red lights ahead of you wouldn't surprise you.

In the City of Angels after midnight, there are plenty of folks heading home from the late shift or getting an early start to the morning commute. I also piggybacked on the popularity of being on the No. 1-rated music station in L.A. Many commuters looking for great rock music to keep them energized and alert on the freeways tuned into 95.5 FM.

Man, did it feel good to have my own talk show gig in radio. After decades of being put down and made fun of by my contemporaries, after fifteen years of stocking shelves in the supermarket business, and after bouncing on freeway pavement like a crash dummy, I finally showed everyone that I could amount to something. All of Southern California was within the sound of my voice, which was a wonderfully exciting thought. I really believed radio was my destiny.

Maybe I wasn't ready for prime time, but I felt confident enough to hold my own on a talk show that aired in the middle of the night. If given half the chance, I believed I could engage and hold an audience through my people skills and verbosity. In a way, I felt that establishing a connection with my listeners was no different than making a connection with a lonely soul passing through my checkstand.

I knew I could talk glibly about spirituality and things that matter after apprenticing with Michael Benner, gaining knowledge from life-changing books like actress Shirley MacLaine's *Out on a Limb*, and attending lectures by spiritual luminaries such as Scottish author and esotericist Benjamin Creme. These experiences gave me the necessary gravitas to shed light on a variety of topics that nearly everyone was interested in.

If you were fascinated by the supernatural, I was your guy. If you were turned off by organized religion, you had a home. If you were a seeker, you could find answers to your simple or difficult questions. If you were a fellow traveler on this journey called life, I had your back. As far as I was concerned, we were all on a quest to make sense of the world around us.

Right from the start of my radio career, I decided that I would be as transparent as possible. When appropriate to the topic on hand, I spoke of my own journey to find truth, using my motorcycle crash as a springboard to a discussion of how that traumatic event took me to a higher plane of consciousness.

When I was taking call after call, no matter what topic or tangent we were on, I felt like I was doing what I was supposed to do, which was to facilitate an open-ended discussion of the spirit world. Like my predecessor, I employed the stock phrases to describe this phenomenon: human potential, self-improvement, and positive thinking.

The Harmonic Convergence in the summer of 1987 is when the term "New Age" came into vogue. The mainstream media was searching for a label to pin on spiritual-minded folks who had turned their backs on organized religion and denominational churches, and they came up with New Age.

At the time, though, I didn't want to pigeonhole myself into a certain spiritual box. I wanted to be all things to all spiritually minded people. But looking back through the prism of time, the *Impact* show *was* New Age, as the term is commonly understood today. What I was doing was tapping into folks who were open to hearing about alternatives to organized religion. These non-conformist practices included meditation, channeling, crystal healing, psychic experiences, astral projection, and reincarnation.

To be conversant on this wide range of topics, I studied every subject and spiritual quest I could, which wasn't easy in those pre-Google days. If I couldn't do the matter justice, then I asked listeners to enlighten me. The way I saw things, every Sunday night was like hosting a class in spirituality; I was the facilitator, and my listening audience were the students. Or the adjunct professors on occasion.

After a couple of years at KLOS, your humble host started receiving invitations to speak at Whole Life Expos that featured a hodgepodge of alchemists, palm readers, and crystal-toting seekers. I readily accepted, grateful for the chance to promote *Impact* but also have my ego stroked. Standing before an audience and hearing myself talk about ways to realize your human potential to dozens or hundreds of people was a dream come true. One of the proudest days was when a *Los Angeles Times* writer referred to me as a "New Age guru." I took that as a compliment and testimony that I had finally arrived.

I was a spiritual tutor. A teacher raising consciousness. A sage of the Southwest.

I really believed I had found my place.

ASCENDED MASTERS

As far as I was concerned, I wasn't going to leave any stone unturned in my show prep or in any topic relating to spirituality. A colleague told me that I should check into Samadhi Flotation Tanks, which are also known as sensory deprivation tanks. Samadhi was a Sanskrit word that meant a state of deep contemplation leading to extraordinary lucidity, concentration, and deep meditation. If a flotation tank could do that for me, I was all ears, even if I got wet.

I checked the Yellow Pages for Samadhi Flotation Tanks and found several "light centers" in West Los Angeles advertising their availability. One afternoon, I visited a place named Altered States and gave sensory deprivation a try. A little larger than a twin-sized bed, a float tank contained ten inches of water that was saturated in an Epsom salt solution—something like five hundreds pounds worth of salts. When I crept in on all fours and laid on my back, I floated like a cork. The effect was similar to the weightlessness that an astronaut experiences in space, which made sense. Physician and neuroscientist John Lilly invented flotation tanks in the late 1950s, just before the dawn of the Space Age.

The sensation of floating in water heated to body temperature in total darkness was a tremendous feeling, and for the next year or two, I was a regular at Altered States. I really liked slipping into a calm relaxed state that helped me lose all reference to where I was. I usually floated for an hour, which gave me enough time to reach a state where all my senses shut down. Not only was it great for my body to experience near weightlessness, but the calming experience allowed my mind to reach a near meditative state.

During that time, I read a book on flotation tanks by author Ken Hutchinson, who believed that people with broken bones—a leg, an arm—healed faster when they floated consistently in a sensory deprivation tank over a two-week period. The theory behind this was that bones healed faster because there was no gravity working on the bones knitting together, which accelerated the healing process. Since I thought there was something there, I talked about sensory deprivation tanks on *Impact* and asked to hear from listeners about their experiences.

When I wasn't facilitating important discussions, I loved bringing compelling guests on to the show. Perhaps the iconic in-studio guest for me was Benjamin Creme, who I could count on to light up the call-in lines. Creme was in his mid-sixties when I became host of *Impact*. With his halo of white hair, clipped British accent, and authoritative air, he looked and sounded like someone who knew the spiritual world well.

His story began in 1959 when he was contacted by one of the "Ascended Masters" who told Benjamin via "telepathic communication" that he had a mission similar to John the Baptist, and that was to prepare the way for the coming of Lord Maitreya, an Ascended Master who would assume human form and prepare humankind for the coming of the Age of Aquarius, which was known in New Age circles as a time of peace, plenty, and perfect equality.

I was drawn to Benjamin's message because he said that during the Age of Aquarius, governments around the world would share and equally distribute the goods of the world through the global governance of the United Nations. A one-world, one-government future sounded like the direction this troubled planet needed to go to my progressive-minded audience and me.

Benjamin, when he took a seat in the studio, was most animated when talking about Lord Maitreya. Seeking to build wide support for his case, he said that Lord Maitreya has been expected to come to earth by followers of all of the major religions. Christians knew Maitreya as Jesus

Christ, who was prophesied to return again as part of the Second Coming. Jews awaited for their Messiah. Hindus were told to expect the coming of Krishna, while Buddhists referred to this holy figure as Maitreya Buddha. Muslims anticipated the Twelfth Imam or Mahdi.

The name may be different, but Benjamin believed they referred to the same individual. He declared that Lord Maitreya would come as a teacher and guide to people of every religion *and* those of no religion. According to Benjamin, Lord Maitreya would inspire humanity to see itself as one family and create a civilization based on sharing and economic and social justice. Adequate food, housing, clothing, education, and medical care would become universal rights.

I remember asking Creme when Lord Maitreya came to be. According to this British teacher of esoteric philosophy, Lord Maitreya was already among us. He descended from his ancient retreat in the Himalayas in July 1977 and took up residence in the Indian-Pakistani community in London. He was living and working there just like any ordinary bloke, his true status known only to a few like Benjamin Creme. Lord Maitreya, he said, was waiting until just the right time to demonstrate his true identity.

I didn't buy everything that Benjamin said hook, line, and sinker, but he was such a sweet guy with beautiful eyes and a gentle spirit that I couldn't help but be enthralled by his presence. We became very good friends. He flew in from London twice a year to lecture and make appearances in the Los Angeles area. He had a standing invitation to come by the KLOS studios off La Cienega on Sunday nights. Something that impressed me was that he took no money from his lectures. He lived on a meager salary, which meant his motives were pure.

Another altruistic person who received a lot of airtime on my show was Bo Lozoff, who founded the Human Kindness Foundation, a great name for a nonprofit organization whose signature outreach was known as the Prison-Ashram Project. Bo's ministry mailed free interfaith books, CDs, and correspondence to prisoners around the world.

Bo and a spiritual teacher named Ram Dass, who originally came up with the idea for the Prison-Ashram Project, wanted to help convicts view their prison as an ashram instead of seeing themselves as prisoners marking time until they were released. *Ashram* is a Sanskrit word meaning "house of God," and in Eastern religion, an ashram is a place where people live for a period of time to strengthen their spiritual practice and self-discipline. By getting prisoners to view their cells like ashrams—a place for spiritual growth—they would have greater hope for the future.

Bo's book, *We're All Doing Time*, was widely referred to as the "convict's Bible." He traveled around the world to give talks in hundreds of prisons, churches, and community centers. He'd say that it was easy getting wrapped up in the spiritual "search" and losing sight of the fact that the search was an inner journey. The greatest discoveries in life were made when we learned how to be perfectly still so that we could experience silence of body, silence of speech, and silence of mind. Bo said that Buddha called this the "noble silence."

Although Bo presented himself as an "interfaith" teacher, he was an Eastern religion guy. The major reason I identified with him was how he started his spiritual journey, which began at the age of eighteen when he was involved in a terrific car crash. A momentary lapse of concentration resulted in his vehicle smashing into the back of an eighteen-wheeler. Months of painful surgery and rehabilitation led him on a search for answers to the Big Whys: *Why are we here? Why do we suffer?*

Bo and I would share our stories and bat those questions around like croquet balls on a grassy pitch. I felt like a kindred spirit was in the studio whenever he was in L.A. on a speaking tour or visiting prisons.

OTHER PATHS TO GOD

While Bo and Benjamin Creme were mainstream in the world of New Age, I didn't mind shaking things up with the paranormal. One of those was an eccentric scientist and author named Jonathan Vos Post. He would discuss his book, *Me Human, You Alien: How to Talk to an Extraterrestrial*, while I, the *Impact* host, conducted the interview. He said the way to initiate contact with an extraterrestrial was to have the following on hand:

- eighteen specific U.S. coins, totaling $3.27
- a loop of string at least four feet long but no longer than six feet
- a pocket flashlight
- two small bar magnets
- a pad of paper and a couple of pens and pencils
- a camera or a recorder so that you can photograph and/or tape your Close Encounter

Vos Post said the eighteen coins were meant to show the extra-terrestrial, or ET, where we were in the universe. A Susan B. Anthony dollar coin was the sun and surrounded by Mercury (a penny); Venus (a nickel); Earth (another nickel, circled by the Moon, which was a dime); Mars, a penny, and so on down the line. If you met an extraterrestrial, you were to lay out the coins in such a manner. If it was daytime, then you were supposed to point to the sun and say, "Sun!" and then point to the second nickel and say "Earth!" Then Vos Post recommended turning silent, backing away from the coins, and watching for a response. "It" may construct a model of its own solar system. If that happens, Vos Post said, be sure to take photos since those images and information may be worth millions of dollars beyond your original outlay of $3.27.

I did a lot of shows on UFOs because my interest in unidentified flying objects dated back to when my parents would take me out to actor Jack Palance's ranch in Tehachapi ninety minutes northeast of the Valley. Jack was a great actor whose most famous roles were as the craggy-faced menace in the 1950s movie *Shane* and as tough-as-cowhide Curly Washburn in the comedy *City Slickers* from the early '90s. After winning the Oscar for Best Supporting Actor for his role in *City Slickers*, he dropped to the stage and performed one-handed push-ups at the age of seventy-three.

The reason my parents knew Jack was not from Dad's work on the set but because the famous actor's brother, John, was married to Mom's cousin Rita. I called him "Uncle Jack."

One time, we were invited out to his ranch in Tehachapi even though Uncle Jack was on location somewhere. That night, we walked the "back forty" and saw a lot of weird stuff in the heavens. I distinctly remember a couple of adults pointing out several UFOs floating above the rural skies of Tehachapi. At least, that's what I thought all the lights in the sky were—unidentified flying objects.

Another UFO event that sticks out in my mind happened on April 1, 1966, and it was no April Fools joke. My mom's brother, Uncle Tony, lived in the San Fernando Valley and was as Italian as they come. We were hanging out in his backyard one night. On the horizon, four UFOs hovered in the distance. Uncle Tony saw them first and yelled at everybody to look to the sky.

I was ten years old, so this was just about the most exciting thing that ever happened to me in my life. I watched the lead UFO track against the nighttime upper atmosphere, followed by three others UFOs in formation.

No vapor trail, no sound.

During my first few years on *Impact*, I brought a lot of ufologists onto the show to discuss either what they saw or their theories. I generally accepted everything they said as the gospel truth. Something was out there, right? That was my guiding worldview at the time.

Another New Age thing like astral projection, which is defined as being able to separate from the physical body and travel outside of those norms, fascinated me. I had people come on the show and claim that 5 to 10 percent of the world's population had been part of a conscious out-of-body experience and that it was possible to teach yourself how to hover above your bed when you were in a deep sleep. Like anything, it just took some practice.

One of the controversial areas of New Age was a practice called channeling, which is defined as a natural form of communication between humans and angelic beings, nature spirits, non-physical entities, and even animals and pets. Another way to look at channelers is to see them as translators or interpreters of what entities are saying in the spirit world.

When I started on *Impact* in 1987, channeling was the rage in New Age thinking. The face of channeling was a Seattle woman named JZ Knight, who channeled a spiritual entity named Ramtha. Perhaps you remember seeing a feature on *20/20* or some other newsmagazine show about JZ Knight, an attractive blonde in her mid-thirties with striking blue eyes. She also appeared on talk shows like the *Merv Griffin Show* and *Larry King Live*.

The metamorphosis from JZ Knight, who looked like a soccer mom, to Ramtha, a 35,000-year-old spirit warrior who spoke mostly in English with a guttural, husky accent that sounded like an Indian raj, was something else to witness, which I did on numerous occasions. JZ Knight was too big in the late 1980s and early 1990s to bother coming on a radio program that started at midnight, but I made sure I saw her speak in person. Ms. Knight claimed to have lived many lives, which I found fascinating because reincarnation made sense to me. I always wondered what I had done in a past life that was so bad that it earned me a messed-up childhood and a life-altering motorcycle accident.

MORE ENERGY POINTS

One night, I had a scientist and futurist named Stephen Schwartz on the show. As research director and chairman of the Mobius Society, his field of expertise was a practice called "remote viewing." As far as I was concerned, this was a meaty topic. Remote viewing is when you seek impressions about somebody or something through ESP, or extra-sensory perception. Remote viewers can see objects or scenes hundreds or thousands of miles away by closing their eyes and focusing on an object or place.

How does that happen? You begin your remote viewing experience by turning your mind into something like an empty rice bowl, which is another way of saying that you relax, close your eyes, breathe deeply, and empty your mind. Then you look for the black window in your mind that you can gaze into.

You will see images come forth, but they will probably be indistinct shapes and colors. If that happens, you're coached to relax even more and continue to empty your mind. Soon, you should receive remote viewing signals as your imagination roams like a cell phone in the middle of the Mojave Desert. When I worked at Ralph's, I really felt like there were times when I could tell what shoppers were thinking as they strolled through the aisles, plucking food items off the shelves.

Chakras, or energy points on the body, were another topic that I loved to explore. The body has seven chakras, beginning with the chakra at the base of your spine. After chakras, the body has energy meridians, which have their basis in Chinese medicine. We had a guest one time describe how the twelve meridians of the body—which are the lungs, large intestine, stomach, spleen, heart, small intestine, bladder, kidney, heart governor, triple heater, gall bladder and liver—affect every organ and physiological system inside of us. Meridians carry energy and were referred to as *chi, qi,* or *prana.* I loved hearing how meridians bring vitality and balance.

Energy meridians made sense to me because of acupuncture treatments I underwent after my motorcycle crash. Each pin that punctured my skin opened a blocked meridian. One of the key underpinnings of New Age thinking, besides that there are many paths to God, is that we are energy beings. Our challenge is to learn how to harness, channel, and increase that energy.

One other aspect to New Age that I explored was how the brain contributes to your state of mind. Different brain waves, or frequencies, travel through the circuitry inside the brain at speeds we can't comprehend. These brain waves are called Beta, Alpha, Theta, and Delta, and their frequency could be measured in cycles per second. Here are the differences between the four kinds of brain waves:

- Beta brain waves are associated with normal daily activity and carry a heightened state of alertness, logic, and critical reasoning.
- Alpha brain waves happen when your eyes are closed and you're daydreaming or performing light meditation. Your capacity for imagination and visualization are foremost in this state.
- Theta brain waves come forth when you're in deep meditation or sleeping lightly. For example, a Theta frequency cycle is similar to the constant and rhythmic drone of Tibetan Buddhist monks chanting in a way that allows them to step into the realms of blissful meditation.
- Delta brain waves are the slowest and are associated with how your brain behaves when you're in a deep sleep.

I could recite the cycles per second for each of the four brain wave activities. A Beta frequency ranged between 14 to 40 cycles per second, or Hz; a higher number was a sign of considerable stress in one's life. Those able to lower their brain waves to the Alpha level (7.5 to 14 Hz) were in a more relaxed state.

Everything I read about Theta brain waves (between 4.7 and 5.0 Hz) said this was the state you wanted to be in, where a deep spiritual connection could be experienced through deep meditation. The hallmark for Theta brain waves was vivid visualizations, meaningful inspiration, keen creativity, and unprecedented insights.

I resolved to give myself a half hour each day, at a minimum, to tap into Alpha brain waves, which was the relaxed, optimum place to be.

THE LEADING EDGE OF TRUTH

As I got deeper into New Age philosophy, I came to a point where I believed that there were so many aspects to this new way of thinking that it would be impossible to set limits on what the mind and the body were capable of. No matter what, I had to keep exploring what was out there. I had to make my mind wide open to the possibilities of the universe. Only then could I be on the vanguard of societal evolution—the leading edge of truth.

I left no stone unturned in this quest. I read Hindu texts like the

Bhagavad Gita, which was comprised of 700 verses of scripture that were part of the bigger Hindu epic known as the Mahabharata. The *Bhagavad Gita* was set in a narrative framework, the related dialogue being between a Pandava prince named Arjuna and his guide Lord Krishna. I received "ageless wisdom" from reading this text.

I was also quite familiar with the *Upanishads*, a collection of Vedic texts that described the central religious concepts of Hinduism, Buddhism, and Jainism. For good measure, I also familiarized myself with the Quran, which was the foundation of the Islamic faith. Quranic chapters were called *suras,* and verses were called *ayahs*. I will confess that the Five Pillars of Islam—testifying there is no God but Allah and Muhammad is his prophet; praying five times a day; giving to charity; fasting during the month of Ramadan; and making the Hajj pilgrimage to Mecca at least once in a lifetime—were a bridge too far for me. But to each his own, I figured.

While I wasn't on board with the Five Pillars, I certainly respected the central religious text of Islam. The way I viewed things, the sheer number of Muslim adherents worldwide—1.6 billion or 23 percent of the world's population—meant that I couldn't ignore this spiritual tradition. Even though Christians were the only religious group to outnumber Muslims (with 2.2 billion, or 32 percent of the world's population), they didn't count. I had a blind spot when it came to Christianity, based on how I had seen Mom's Catholic faith let her down with Dad. That's the major reason why I wouldn't open a Bible. I wanted nothing to do with that book. And if someone spouted Bible verses on the show, I loved yanking the caller off the air.

So I knew a lot about religion and spirituality. I was not so full of myself to think that I had all the answers, but as a dedicated student of all things spiritual with his own radio show in a major U.S. city, I was closer to finding truth—and my bliss—than most people. That's why I felt comfortable being a teacher to every person who tuned into *Impact* each week.

The way I saw things, they were my flock, and I was their shepherd.

14

RUNNING ON EMPTY

A month after the Harmonic Convergence in August 1987, a differ-ent kind of spirit fell on Los Angeles. I'm talking about the *Mark & Brian Show*, which began airing on KLOS from 6-10 a.m. during the Monday-through-Friday morning commute.

The show's freewheeling mix of sexually explicit and scatological humor, biting satire, anything-goes commentary, prank phone calls, and clever comedy "bits" were quite a departure from the station's classic rock format. Normally, L.A. commuters tuning into KLOS heard one great rock song after another with minimal talk from the on-duty jock. That all changed, though, when Mark Thompson and Brian Phelps rolled into town from Birmingham, Alabama, where their "morning zoo" format had been a ratings hit.

Would their comedy shtick work in Southern California?

They were pushing the envelope to find out. Mark and Brian were part of the latest wave in radio—the rise of "shock jocks." Their mission was to titillate, entertain, and surprise their audience with an R-rated blend of raunchy material, bawdy song parodies, goofy pranks, leering gags, and ribald jokes that kept ears tuned in during the morning drive time. Their gig was helped by the Federal Communications Commis-sion's decision to loosen its definition of what constituted radio indecency during the 1980s. Once the FCC opened the floodgates, naughty DJs in every major market rushed in like the Johnstown flood. Boundary lines were obliterated.

Many edgy jocks were two-man teams like "Bob & Tom" at WFBQ in Indianapolis or "Don & Mike" from WJFK in the Washington, D.C. metro area, but the 800-pound gorilla of the genre was Howard Stern of WXRK in New York City. His weekday show also aired in a handful of other cities via syndication. Stern's nasally voice and unfiltered mouth invariably veered in the direction of sex, farting, belching, and other sophomoric stunts. He and his radio confederates across the fruited plain happily stomped on FCC decency regulations with provocative programming that greatly appealed to the "frat boy" side of the coveted 18-34 male demographic, as they say in radiospeak.

In the early going, the KLOS audience didn't like the *Mark & Brian Show* because they wanted to hear classic rock standards on the way to work, not listen to a couple of guys joking about their sexual fantasies or wondering what the proper amount was to tip lap dancers. This was similar to the reaction that I received when KLOS listeners didn't immediately warm to me taking Michael Benner's place on *Impact*.

Within six months or so, though, Mark and Brian's talent to make people laugh found an audience—a healthy one. It didn't take them long to supplant the No. 1-rated show hosted by Rick Dees, a lively, fast-paced DJ playing Top 40 hits at KIIS-FM, 102.7 on the dial.

Mark and Brian, who wore fashionable mullets in the early days—business up front, party in the back—weren't Howard Stern clones. They took great pains to distinguish themselves from the brash East Coast entertainer with a mop of unruly curls. Mark Thompson, who started his radio career as a sixteen-year-old sweeping up the studio at a station in his hometown of Florence, Alabama, was the natural straight man for Brian Phelps, a tall, blond comedy club performer from the Midwest who was a very funny guy with a knack for character voices.

Because this is a family book, I won't share graphic examples of their sex-drenched spectacle. Trust me, they got pretty descriptive. Their act was filled with jokes about male and female genitalia, every type of sex act under the sun, and double entendres that busted themselves and their audience into bouts of chortling and chuckling. I'll admit that I laughed my butt off like everyone else.

Some of the crazy things I can tell you about were when they prompted a pregnant woman in her ninth month to call her unavailable husband

and pretend she was going into full-bore labor at that very moment. Mark and Brian thought it would be funny to hear the guy's panicked reaction. Of course, the father-to-be didn't know half of L.A. was listening in.

Another time, they persuaded singer Barry White—owner of one of the deepest voices in pop music—to take a whiff of helium and talk like a Munchkin from "The Wizard of Oz." For a Valentine's Day stunt one year, Mark and Brian organized a giant vat of soft chocolate to be delivered to the station parking lot. A rented crane lowered the pair into the tub of liquid chocolate while onlookers threw nuts and toppings on them.

The show was totally live. They made up stuff as they went along, but Brian also wrote scripted material, or "bits." The guy was a genius. One time, he made fun of the rock group Crosby, Stills, Nash & Young because they were always touring with different permutations of the four musicians. With "Our House" and "Suite: Judy Blue Eyes" playing in the background, Mark and Brian took turns breathlessly announcing their latest concert swing through Southern California in this mock advertisement:

> **Mark:** *Here's your chance to see them live, March 25 in Long Beach—it's Crosby and Nash! It used to be Crosby, Stills, and Nash and Crosby, Stills, Nash, & Young, but now it's just Crosby and Nash.*

> **Brian:** *But now, on March 28, in Anaheim, it's Nash! Yes, it's finally your chance to see Graham Nash on his own, without those other guys slowing him down.*

> **Mark:** *But on March 30, in Pasadena, it's the Graham Nash Tribute band, Nam Grash! It's Nam Grash, the ultimate Graham Nash tribute band that sounds exactly like Nash.*

> **Brian:** *But on April 2 in Chino, it's the Nam Grash Tribute Band Must Nash! Not to be confused with Moustache, Must Nash plays all the must-have hits of Graham Nash, but their sound is slightly more Nam Grash than Graham Nash.*

> **Mark:** *And on April 5 in Burbank, it's Graham Nash lookalike Stan Bash watching an episode of Nash Bridges on an episode of "MASH"!*

> **Brian:** *Stan Bash doesn't sound like Graham Nash or Nam Grash but he looks exactly like Nash frontman and former Crosby and Nash, Crosby, Stills, and Nash, and Crosby, Stills, Nash, and Young member Graham Nash.*

> **Mark:** *When old rockers stick around for forty years, this kind of crap is going to happen.*

Okay, that's an example of their tame stuff. Believe me, they ran with the racy material most of the time, mining anything to do with sex for a good laugh. The whole idea was to keep people tuning in, and let's face it—talking about something to do with sex was a winner in those days when no one had done it before. They also wanted listeners to wonder what crazy stunt was coming up next or what lunatic prank they'd pull.

Since the three of us all got our starts on KLOS in the fall of 1987, I felt a kinship with Mark and Brian. I really wanted them to succeed. Our paths crossed every Monday morning in the pre-dawn hours when I signed off *Impact* at 5 a.m. while they were doing show prep prior to their six o'clock start. I'd listen to them on my way home and laugh out loud because they were darn funny. Their rise in the ratings was slow and steady. Within three years after arriving in the Southland, Mark and Brian were the toast of L.A. morning radio.

I was happy for Mark and Brian and for the station. As the saying goes, a rising tide lifts all boats. Even if the KLOS ship motored its way through sludge-infested waters when Mark and Brian were at the helm, their success made a lot of money for the station and lifted the morale of everyone working at KLOS.

CONTROLLING THE BOARD

When I started jocking at KLOS on Friday and Saturday nights, part of my reason for taking the gigs was to show the station bosses that I was more than a one-trick New Age pony. I wanted to demonstrate that I could do more than rattle on about spirituality or environmentalism until the roosters started crowing. From the professional side of the microphone,

I made smooth, no-mistake transitions in and out of commercials and fluidly moved back into music when coming out of those breaks. I also learned how to engineer a show by running the control board, which plays the music, commercials, and PSAs—the public service announcements. The control board is the backbone of any radio show.

Not long after the *Mark & Brian Show* hit No. 1, I stopped working at KZTR in Ventura. A couple of years working seven days a week had emptied the tank, but I was glad to net all that experience. One week, the *Mark & Brian* news director, Chuck Moshantz, happened to be taking some vacation time. "News director" is a fancy title for the person who reads the news breaks three times an hour. The KLOS program director asked me if I'd be interested in filling in. I said sure, even though I had no news reading experience. How hard could it be doing a minute or two of news every twenty minutes?

I found out news reading was harder than it looked because I had to *write* the "news and views" as well. Fortunately, in radio, two or three sentences are about all you need. What I did was lay out the *Los Angeles Times* and the *Valley News* on a back table and clip stories that I thought would be interesting to our listening audience. Then I cobbled together a couple of sentences summing up the salient news peg in each story and typed them out. Even a college dropout like me could do that.

I liked being on the air with Mark and Brian, who often found something to make fun of after I finished reading the news straight. If a politician resigned for some sort of sexual peccadillo or a celebrity was caught cheating on a paramour, they got the full monty treatment from the comedic duo. One time, one of the guys took a match to the news copy I was reading while I was on the air. I held on to the burning page as long as I could and then ad-libbed as the flaming piece of paper hit the floor.

Filling in for a week here and a week there as Mark and Brian's news guy was enjoyable, but I hated waking up at 3:30 a.m. I wanted to throw the alarm clock against the wall each time the loud buzzer startled me out of a deep sleep. I couldn't see living these hours the rest of my life.

Around the same time I lent a hand on the *Mark & Brian Show*, Howard Stern shook up the radio landscape when he moved into the L.A. radio market in 1991. The Los Angeles station, KLSX, 97.1 FM, syndicated his New York show in the same 6-10 a.m. local time slot, so Howard was going head-to-head against Mark and Brian. While one could say that our guys' sex-obsessed joking and good-time banter were juvenile in delivery and taste, Stern's was X-rated adult—basically auditory porn.

The battle lines were drawn: reigning champions Mark and Brian versus challenger Howard Stern. This was a clash for radio supremacy, an all-out war made personal by Stern, who announced that he was out to bury Mark and Brian in the ratings. Shortly after his entry into the L.A. market, Stern staged a contest, asking people to come up with parody songs mocking the KLOS duo. Flo and Eddie of the Sixties' group, The Turtles, and friends of Stern, responded by redoing "Happy Together" as "So Crappy Together"—referring to Mark and Brian.

The Turtles' song was merely the opening salvo. The Fartman, as the L.A. media nicknamed him, kept up the nasty stunts until he surpassed Mark and Brian in the ratings. To celebrate his triumph—and figuratively spike the football in the end zone—Stern flew out from New York and staged a "mock funeral" on Hollywood Boulevard that was a media spectacle in itself. Dressed like a Roman emperor and standing triumphant before a blood-thirsty crowd of 5,000, Stern ordered two minions to drag effigies of Mark and Brian to a guillotine, where they were decapitated amid raucous cheers.

All this craziness was swirling around when Rita Wilde, Mark and Brian's program director, asked me if I would be interested in becoming the show engineer, which meant running their control board. I knew this assignment would be a lot different than ripping and reading the news. Running Mark and Brian's control board presented me with an opportunity to do something new in radio—and be really hands-on with the show. I'd be inside the studio and sitting across the table from Mark and Brian, operating the control board that produced the show's music, special sound effects, and commercials. I would have a mic as well, which meant I could be part of the on-the-air mix, a sidekick to the two stars. Kind of like an Ed McMahon to Johnny Carson.

"The guys love you," Rita said. "They said you got along great with them when you filled in. They're picky with who they want to work with."

It didn't take long for me to formulate a reply.

"Absolutely not," I said. I was doing four KLOS shows on the weekends, doing New Age lectures on weeknights, and making the odd appearance at health-and-wellness expos. The last thing I wanted to do was get up at 3:30 in the morning five days a week and get involved in that morning bedlam. I had my own thing going. I was happy.

Rita understood my reluctance and accepted my explanation. Then she asked me for a favor. "Would you fill in for a month while we bring in some people to audition?"

Like a good soldier, I said yes. One month turned into three months as Mark and Brian auditioned various folks to engineer their show. They couldn't find anybody they liked. The guys hated everyone who tried out and even made fun of their mistakes on the air.

After three months, Rita took a different approach. "We want to offer you a contract," she said. Hearing that caught my attention. I had never had a contract at that point. KLOS, like I said before, was a union shop, so I was paid a union wage to do the weekend shows. I didn't have what is known in the industry as a "personal services" contract.

This time, the higher-ups at KLOS were offering me a handsome salary to sign me for three years. My reply: "I think I can get up at 3:30 in the morning for that kind of money." While the earnings bump was appreciated, it was probably one-twentieth of what Mark and Brian were knocking down, but I was okay with that. Hey, it was their show and their ratings.

I also felt a certain amount of comfort with Mark Thompson and Brian Phelps. I was the same age as Mark and three years older than Brian, so we were on the same generational wavelength. I didn't mind the sexual humor, although I remember one time they ambushed the staff—on the air—by asking us what sexual acts we had never participated in but would like to try. I kept my head down and passed on that one, but off-the-wall stuff like that shows you how things got pretty steamy inside the studio.

When they broached safer topics and I was invited to participate, I contributed to the witty repartee. If Mark and Brian used me as a foil to get some laughs, I figured that was part of my job description. They pigeonholed me as the New Age guy, which opened the door to jokes like this:

What do you get when you play New Age music backwards?

Answer: New Age music.

They also teased me about how I was getting thin on top. My days of wearing my hair down to my shoulders were rapidly closing. One morning, Brian proposed shaving off all of my hair—on the air. Of course, the audience couldn't see what was happening, but that would be one more example of how the "theater of the mind" worked. I said sure, why not? One morning, after a proper build-up, I let them fuss over me as the shaving cream was applied. A few minutes of razor work is all it took for me to have the Kojak look that I have today.

Being part of the *Mark & Brian Show* had other benefits. My ratings as the *Impact* host on Sunday nights shot up, pleasing the powers that be at KLOS. My seminars grew from the extra exposure. As I settled in for a long run with Mark and Brian, I stopped jocking on Friday nights and Saturday nights but I still did the double-up on Sundays—hosting *Impact* from midnight to 5 a.m. and moving right into *Mark & Brian* an hour later, taking my place behind the control board. Mondays were long days.

As they say in show business, working with these funny, inventive guys was the start of a beautiful friendship. I got used to the grind of waking up at 3:30 in the morning. You blink your eyes, and three years go by like that. Along came another three-year contract, and off we'd go.

ALL ABOUT THE MONEY

The success of the *Mark & Brian Show* was nice, but I wasn't caught up in the fame and money. Why? Because I was more spiritual than the next person. I viewed myself as a virtuous soul uninterested in temporal pursuits. I wasn't into material possessions. A higher level of consciousness held more importance, as well as my relationships with women.

I've already mentioned how I fathered Lindsay Sontag in 1988, shortly after I started with KLOS. Her mother, Karen, and I tried to make things work, but we got into a physical altercation one day, which triggered bad memories of my father getting aggressively physical with me. I didn't need that, so I moved out and met with a marriage counselor to sort out what happened. This was the counselor who recommended that I move back in and be a father to Lindsay until she was at least four years old.

After she turned four, I plotted my exit strategy. I had to leave Karen because I couldn't hack it any longer. We got a legal separation that sent us down a path toward divorce.

In June 1992, a few months after Lindsay's fourth birthday, I was lecturing at the Philosophical Research Society, a block-like center and library on Los Felix near the Greek Theater. Manly P. Hall, a Canadian-born author and mystic, founded the Philosophical Research Society in 1934, dedicating the non-profit organization to, in his own words, "the teachings of lost and hidden traditions, the golden verses of Hindu gods, Greek philosophers and Christian mystics, and the spiritual treasures waiting to be found within one's own soul." Hall was an ordained preacher with Church of the People whose seminal book, *The Secret Teachings of All Ages*, was a grab bag of Hermetic doctrine, the workings of Kabbalah, the meaning of cryptograms, the symbols of Rosicrucianism, and the significance of Native American spirits, just to name a few of his spiritual leanings.

I was down with all that. Free thinking was the goal of this institution that rejected doctrinal, political, and ecclesiastical artifices but provided a safe haven and learning environment sheltered from any intention to coerce or convert.

I booked speaking engagements twice month at the Philosophical Research Society, usually on Monday nights. Audiences ranging from fifty to one hundred souls were hungry for answers to philosophical questions in their mind. As far as I was concerned, they came to the right place. The Greek word *philosophy* came from *phileo*, meaning "love," and *sophia*, meaning "wisdom." The seekers who came to the Philosophical Research Society were seeking the wisdom of the ages, and I really thought I could be a knowledgeable conduit to truth.

The Philosophical Research Society wasn't a bad place to seek out women, either. After I moved out on Karen and Lindsay, that's where I met Jennie (not her real name) after one of my lectures at PRS.

I fell hard for her, but she played hard to get. Part of that was because she was an aspiring actress trying to break into Hollywood, so she was focused on casting calls and learning lines. We dated off and on for the better part of a year, and I even tried to talk her into moving in with me. I was living in a rent-controlled apartment in Santa Monica at the time, a convenient twenty-minute commute to the KLOS studio at four in the morning.

She resisted. Jennie had a good job working as a hostess at a Hollywood nightclub, in the VIP section. She made a ridiculous amount of money in cash tips, sometimes as much as $500 a night. But after developing breathing problems from all the excessive cigarette smoking, she was forced to quit working at the nightclub. When money got tight for her, she agreed to move in with me and eventually began working with me at KLOS as my screener on *Impact*.

I'm compressing some details here, but a few years later, I asked: "Will you marry me?" She said yes. We exchanged vows before a justice of the peace. Having been together six years at this point, I knew we were right for each other and wanted to see if we could make a marriage work.

Shortly after the wedding, though, Jennie made overtures that marrying me was a mistake. Dissing our marriage complicated matters since we had purchased a home in Granada Hills in the Valley. Jennie persisted in her refrain that we were a bad match and never should have tied the knot. A month later, she took matters into her own hands by packing up and moving back to her old hometown of Monterey, south of San Francisco. Once she arrived up north, I knew the marriage was over. I stayed in our house until we decided when and how to end things. While in Monterey, she hooked up with her childhood boyfriend, but he kicked her out, creating even more drama.

Despite the affair, I wanted her back. After one last trip to Monterey to convince Jennie to return, she said no. She had moved on. As the year 2000 rolled around, Jennie and I were separated but not legally divorced.

Other than that, everything was fine as I entered the new millennium. I was feeling like I was part of the woodwork at KLOS. *Impact* continued to get great ratings for its time slot. I remained a much-in-demand speaker and spoke eloquently about how everything is God and God is everything and how man is God or a part of God—we just didn't know it yet. In addition, I said we can create our own reality and values through transformed consciousness or altered states of consciousness, and it was up to us to seek out those states of consciousness. Lastly, I reiterated my Buddhist-inspired belief that we never die but are reborn over and over until we reach inner peace. The cycle of life and death keeps going and going.

I made good pocket money at my lectures. Since I booked the auditorium, I kept the admission fees, which were either $5 or $10, and sold audiocassette tapes—just like Michael Benner—at the back table. I usually took home between $300 to $1,000 each time I conducted my lectures. I also launched a website as a vehicle to move product. In those early days of e-commerce, I sold more than a few tapes and CDs of my lectures.

If you heard me speak back then, you knew I didn't wing it. I spent a considerable amount of time preparing my remarks, but what I think people related to was my sympathetic manner and empathetic style of communicating. I positioned myself not as a lofty leader above the fray but as a fellow sojourner on a shared path toward the wisdom of the ages.

And then I met Erin Cline at one of my lectures.

15

YEAR OF THE CAT

L et me set the stage:

In 2000, I was separated but not legally divorced from Jennie, who was living in Monterey. I was forty-four years old and had been in radio for thirteen years. Through diligent study and personal search, I had become a respected and thoughtful apologist for a philosophy in which heightened spiritual consciousness led to enlightenment, which ultimately led us all to the God within us. I believed that individuals could experience this enlightenment through personal transformation brought upon by meditative thought and contemplative reflection.

One night, I decided to do a charity event at the Philosophical Research Society on behalf of a cat shelter. I'd say around 150 feline-loving folks showed up inside the main auditorium. During the reception, I shook hands and made small talk with attendees. When I took the podium, I spoke about how homeless cats awaited horrific fates unless we could adequately fund the cat shelter we were supporting that evening. Only then could we prevent needless suffering for the strays among us.

Afterwards, people surrounded me to describe their cat stories or say nice things about listening to me on the *Impact* show. I took their complimentary comments in stride, but I'll admit that my shoulders stiffened in pride. I liked being recognized in the community as a high-minded individual, yea, even a spiritual leader, if I let my mind travel that far.

This was the persona I had worked many years to achieve.

And then Erin Cline introduced herself. She was drop-dead gorgeous, thin as a runway model but carrying a curvy swimsuit figure. Long brown hair, straight. College age.

Attraction bells sounded in my head, even though she was much younger than me. I had always appreciated great beauty, no matter the age.

"I listen to you a lot on KLOS," she said. "I've even called in a couple of times."

"You have? How nice of you to participate in the show," I said. I meant it. I never took listeners for granted. You couldn't, not when your show aired in the middle of the night.

"Yeah, one time you were talking about how there was no benefit in becoming angry, but I didn't like how you were portraying that," she said. "So I called in, and we had a conversation about how to use anger constructively."

I *vaguely* remembered a conversation like that, but I couldn't recall talking to a young woman named Erin about anger issues.

"Oh, yeah. Now I remember. You were a great caller," I said. "We really appreciate it when listeners like you take the trouble to participate in the discussions we have on the show."

There was a knot of people waiting patiently to have a word with me. I had to rush Erin along so I could get to the others, but I didn't want to send her away forever. She was too beautiful.

"Listen, after I'm done here, some of us are going to get a bite to eat. Would you like to join us?"

Her light hazel eyes lit up. "Sure. That sounds like fun."

A half-dozen friends and acquaintances lingered in the main lobby until I finished visiting with everyone who wanted a word with me. When I was done, I slapped my hands together and said, "Whaddya say we go grab something to eat at Shakers in Glendale?"

Shakers was a good half hour from Philosophical Research Society, but most of my friends lived in the Valley, so we would be driving in the right direction. I wasn't sure where Erin lived, though.

"Will Shakers be okay with you?" I asked Erin. I hoped we were going in her direction.

"I live in West Hills," she said. "I'm fine."

Shakers was one of those old-school comfort food diners open till midnight every day. Family owned. Comfortable as an old leather shoe.

I'd been going there for years and liked the food and low-key atmosphere.

It must have been 11 p.m. when we arrived at Shakers. Our large group took possession of a corner booth. My girlfriend at the time sat between Erin and me. While I made sure I paid attention to what both of them had to say, I couldn't keep my eyes off of Erin. When our gaze met, I noticed the mesmerizing energy on both sides.

Don't ask me how I got Erin's phone number before she left with my girlfriend in earshot. I probably thought of some excuse, as in, "Could I call you some time and ask what you think about some of the topics I want to discuss on the show?" I was smitten with her, even though I had a girlfriend that evening. But we weren't that serious. As I recall, we weren't really dating. It was one of those physical relationships.

I waited a few days to call Erin. Total charm offensive. Said I really liked meeting her and would love to see her again. She replied that she'd like to see me, too. We started a relationship that would have more twists and turns than the Matterhorn bobsled run at Disneyland. But at the beginning, I enjoyed discovering this fascinating young woman. Turned out that she had an upbringing that was similar to mine. She was raised a Catholic and had attended parochial schools in the Valley, but after graduating from a Catholic high school, she started looking into Buddhism and a Higher Power. She was on the same search for spirituality as I was, which made us kindred spirits.

When we got together over a bite to eat, I learned that there was a lot more to Erin. I've asked her to share how she grew up, which she agreed to do:

> **Erin:** Like Frank, I grew up in the Valley. My mom, Marylou O'Neil, was born diabetic and was a sickly child growing up in West Hills. She married in her early twenties and tried to make a go of life. Giving birth to me on March 27, 1979—I was her first and only child—must have exacerbated her diabetic symptoms. Right after my birth, Mom lost her eyesight. We moved in with her parents, Dick and Pat Cline, because we had to. Mom couldn't care for me.
>
> Where was my father? He'd show up, and then be gone. I would imagine that having a baby girl and a wife go blind at the same time was just too much to handle.

They separated during my toddler years and divorced when I was around four years old. For all intents and purposes, I didn't have a father growing up. I vaguely remember him being a part of my life.

When I was nine months old, Mom regained 20 percent vision in one eye. That still made her legally blind, but at least she could walk to different rooms or take care of her basic needs. She wasn't an invalid, but because of Mom's disability, she qualified for public assistance, so we moved into a rent-subsidized HUD apartment in nearby Chatsworth. Medi-Cal covered the $327 monthly rent. Social Security, disability, and my grandparents' checks fed us.

It was obvious to Mom's parents that their daughter was overwhelmed by having to raise me. Grandma, a strong, responsible woman who wanted to become a nun growing up, became in many ways the mother I needed. She would pick me up, drive me to school, pick me up when the last school bell rang, feed and clothe me, and care for me for days at a time. Grandma had raised five children and knew what it took to be a mom. I knew she loved me.

My grandfather had a demanding career. He was the successful owner of a chemical engineering firm, so he had a lot on his plate. Being successful, though, afforded them a nice five-bedroom home in West Hills, one of the more affluent suburbs of the San Fernando Valley. I had my own bedroom when I stayed with them. Grandpa and Grandma paid for everything while I grew up—food, housing, private schooling, and clothes.

My grandparents were your typical salt-of-the-earth Irish-Catholic family who made sure we attended Mass on Sunday mornings. When I was old enough to start school, Grandma enrolled me at St. John Eudes School, a private Catholic elementary school in Chatsworth. Grandma wanted me to have a solid Catholic education.

Mom's apartment in Chatsworth was five miles from my grandparent's home in West Hills. Mom did the best she could to raise me, but discipline was more lax than the consistent training and teaching I received in my grandparent's home.

When I stayed in Chatsworth, Mom loved listening to the *Mark & Brian Show* on KLOS each morning as she got me ready to be picked up by my grandmother for school at St. John's. I was eight or nine years old when I first heard Mark and Brian's antics, so this would have been the late '80s when they were getting really popular.

You may be wondering: Wasn't the *Mark & Brian Show* too sexually charged for a third- or fourth-grade girl? Sure it was, but I didn't know any better at the time. My mom was overtly sexual and didn't think it was a bad idea for me to hear about sensual things at my tender age, but listening to the show did sexualize me at an early age. I can remember watching Mark and Brian's short-lived televised comedy show on NBC on Sunday nights with Mom, too. Maybe the laughs we shared took her mind off her troubles, if only for a short moment. What I do know is that we listened religiously to Mark and Brian during my elementary and junior high years.

When I became a freshman, Grandma drove me to Bishop Alemany High School in Mission Hills. She really did a lot for me, especially during my first two years of high school when my world was shook—both literally and figuratively.

The first incident occurred on January 17, 1994, when I was fourteen. A massive 6.7 earthquake, centered underneath the north-central part of the San Fernando Valley, struck at 4:31 in the morning. I was sleeping in Mom's ground-floor apartment in Chatsworth when my bedroom started shaking—violently. The convulsions jostled my bed, and I screamed for my life. The earthquake was so intense that I couldn't get out of my bed; I had to ride it out. When the shaking stopped, I feared that the apartment above us (we lived in a two-story complex) would collapse on me at any moment. I had to get out of there!

But it was pitch black in my bedroom. I crawled toward the door and thought I was about to free myself—when I realized I had crept into my closet. I moved around, and then my dresser fell on top on me. I wasn't crushed, but I struggled to free myself. I screamed for more help.

My mom's boyfriend was living with us. He used his pager to light a path to my bedroom, where he rescued me and got us all to safety in the courtyard. Dozens of shocked residents in various states of undress milled about like zombies. Then I smelled gas! Natural gas! The smell was coming from Chatsworth High School, which was next door. People were saying the buildings were going to blow up any second. Hearing sirens in the distance, seeing the orange glow from burning buildings, not able to go anywhere—this is what I imagined Armageddon to look like. I thought for sure we were doomed.

Gas mains burst and caught on fire. Apartment complexes collapsed and burned. Freeways crumbled. More than sixty died and 9,000 were injured. In my situation, our apartment building was red-tagged, meaning it was deemed uninhabitable to live in. Mom and I moved back in with my grandparents and tried to rebuild our lives.

The other event was more emotional—and was much more difficult for me to handle than a devastating earthquake.

One time after school, Mom showed me an old picture. A man with long, thick brown hair with glasses was staring at the camera.

"That's your father," she said.

I had vague memories of what my father looked like and had seen photos of him before. This person didn't look at all like my father. But the man in the picture had long fingers that matched mine.

"This is your biological father," Mom said.

I still didn't get it, so Mom attempted to explain the situation as best she could. When she was married, she had an affair and got pregnant with me. She was going to leave her husband and marry the man who was my biological father, but he turned abusive on her. So Mom decided to reconcile with her husband, and they agreed to put his name—O'Neil—on my birth certificate.

Except that he was never my real father. Someone else was my father—someone I had never met.

It's hard to describe the emotions I felt as a fifteen-year-old hearing that news. But one thought constantly pounded in my head: *You have no father.*

The hole in my heart confirmed that fathers have an incalculable impact on their daughters. I wasn't mature enough at the time to know that future romantic relationships were influenced positively or negatively by the way a girl interacts with her dad in the childhood years. I had had no such interaction with a male figure when I was growing up.

Not long after Mom gave me the shocking news, my biological father and his wife contacted me from their home in Seattle. We talked on the phone, and they said they wanted to get to know me, but I really did not want any contact with them. They mailed me a short video of themselves and their three sons—my half-brothers—anyway. (Interestingly, my half-brothers and I are very close today.)

Several more months passed before Mom told me that my biological father and his wife were divorcing—and she was moving to Seattle to live with him. Talk about more jolting news. I was glad there was no discussion on whether I wanted to join her in Washington. I wanted to live with Grandma and Grandpa—who had been my main parents most of the time.

That was a rough time. All the foundations of my life were swept away. Losing a home. Changing to a new school campus. Learning about my biological father. My mother moving away to another state. But those were the cards I had been dealt.

Fortunately I had my friends at Alemany High,

which, by the way, was completely destroyed by the Northridge Earthquake, as the media called it. The high school had to be relocated across the street to the campus of Our Lady Queen of Angels Seminary, which caused more upheaval.

Naturally, I sought answers for why all these things were happening. Who was I? Why was I put here on this earth anyway? As I was trying to figure things out, I decided to have my last name legally changed to my grandparents' surname—Cline.

I knew Catholic dogma didn't supply the answers. I needed help because my reality was all over the place as I graduated from high school. Searching for *something* to grasp, I latched onto Buddhism, a path of spiritual development that promised to lead me to insights into the true nature of reality.

Feeling like I was treading water, I enrolled at Pierce College, a two-year community college in nearby Woodland Hills. I got my Associate's degree, but instead of finishing college at a four-year school, I decided to get my California real estate license. I got a position with a local real estate brokerage that did new home sales. I did clerical work and sat on open houses. I liked showing homes.

When I was twenty, I veered away from Buddhism and became interested in Science of Mind, a spiritual, philosophical, and metaphysical religious movement that borrowed the best teachings from the world's great religions. Science of Mind is also known as "Religious Science," and the terms are used interchangeably. The movement did not have churches per se but "Centers for Spiritual Living" that offered participants the necessary spiritual tools to transform their personal lives and make the world a better place. God is not a Supreme Being but a Force.

Science of Mind greatly appealed to me, and I attended their services regularly. What I liked was that all religions were equal, according to Religious Science.

Services started with the lighting of a candle for all the major religions, and what came after that wasn't a sermon but more of a pep talk. I felt like I was connected to a Higher Power. I felt connected to other people, and that made me feel good.

That was the same feeling I got when I listened to *Impact* on KLOS, hosted by a guy named Frank Sontag. I first heard him driving home from a party late on Sunday night because I liked listening to KLOS's album rock when I was driving around. I had fallen out of the habit of listening to the *Mark & Brian Show* because I had outgrown their humor during high school. Plus, after I moved in permanently with my grandparents, I knew this was a show that we were *not* going to listen to while I got ready for school.

I liked what Frank Sontag had to say and started becoming a regular listener of *Impact*. I was a night owl who thought nothing of staying up to two or three in the morning. Sometimes I kept listening until Frank's sign-off at five a.m.

I became part of the community that Frank fostered with the show and appreciated the warm expressions and open demeanor in his voice. I even called in several times to express my point of view. He never argued with me. He'd try to get me to see a different perspective— like the time when I called him about anger. That was fine with me. I saw him as a man of spiritual substance who was on the same wavelength as me.

I was listening the night Frank announced that he would be speaking at a cat shelter fund-raiser at the Philosophical Research Society. I was an animal rights person and loved cats, so I circled the date—December 6, 1999, a Monday. I thought it would be interesting to see what Frank Sontag looked like in the flesh and hear what he had to say in person. After listening to him steadily for more than a year, I imagined him to be in his early forties, short and pudgy and wearing thick bifocals, as befitting a learned man with a powerful intellect. The college professor type with a bow tie.

When I arrived at the Philosophical Research Society, I looked for Frank immediately. Several people were gathered around a tall, muscular bald man who looked like he did a lot of weightlifting. He was casually dressed—a long-sleeved plaid shirt with blue jeans. That had to be Frank's bodyguard. It didn't surprise me that someone as famous as Frank Sontag needed protection. In Los Angeles, it wasn't unusual to see celebrities flanked by a personal bodyguard, so I figured that was the situation here.

When we were asked to take a seat so that the program could start, I was surprised when the bodyguard was introduced as Frank Sontag. I had been wrong, except for his age. The real Frank Sontag wasn't short and squatty and wearing thick glasses. He was tall, handsome, and confident with a pleasant personality. I was impressed. Given our difference in age, I looked up to him, like a student in the presence of a scholarly and highly respected teacher.

I wanted to meet this Frank Sontag, so I waited to have a word with him before I left. When I told him that I had called in before, he said he remembered me, but I could tell he didn't know who I was by the look on his face. How could he remember me? I was just another caller among the hundreds over the years.

That's why I was pleased he asked me to meet him at Shakers. I remember ordering the chocolate brownie dessert at midnight and enjoying being part of this special group. I hung on to his every word.

But if I was really being honest with myself, I was looking for the missing piece in my life.

16

A DAY IN THE LIFE

A few weeks after I met Erin was the start of the new millennium—January 1, 2000. All the Y2K stuff aside, there was a lot of excitement in New Age circles about this momentous date in history. On the *Impact* show, I had guests declare with certainty that we were coming out of the Piscean Age—which started around 200 years BCE (Before Common Era, and don't say "Before Christ")—and moving into the Age of Aquarius, a time of peace and tranquility.

Other experts stated that we were marching into an unprecedented time when we would be ruled by two planets in astrology—Uranus and Saturn. According to these astrology buffs, Uranus represented independence and Saturn represented universal humanism. The humanism philosophy postulated that no dogma or political doctrine could save you: only you could save yourself.

New Age had always been about self—the cornerstone of the movement. In the quest for self-development, self-transformation, self-realization, and self-actualization, if you saved yourself, then you saved Planet Earth.

One thing I wasn't going to save was my marriage to Jennie. When she formally filed for divorce, I let the marriage run its course. Once again, I had failed at matrimony.

Turning my attention to Erin helped me get over this dismal turn of events. Erin made my heart flutter like a schoolboy's, and even better for my sensitive ego, she seemed impressed by me. I could tell she put me on a pedestal. She idolized me. I was fine with that.

Maybe she put me on a pillar, but as we got to know each other better, she found out that I stood on feet of clay—just like any other man. Our dating relationship could be best described as tumultuous. There were hot-and-cold periods of love you/hate you. I don't want to get into particulars, but I could be headstrong in the way I wanted to live, and I'm sure that created needless conflict. I told her about Jennie, so the divorce proceedings hovered over our relationship like a black cloud until the official dissolution decree was issued in 2002.

We had to contend with the difference in age as well. With Erin in her early twenties and me in my mid-forties, I was old enough to be her father. Sometimes I treated her in a condescending manner, as befitting someone older in the relationship.

During our good times, though, the age difference disappeared. I was not the short, squat, middle-aged guy whose dream weekend was watching football games from the couch while munching Cheetos and sipping Bud Light longnecks. I was in excellent physical condition because of a consistent weight-training regimen. More importantly, I liked the trappings of the good life, like eating out at our favorite restaurant, P.F. Chang's, and taking scenic walks on the beach.

After four years of topsy-turvy times, though, we were hanging by a thread. I remember sitting in my car in Santa Monica during one of those up-and-down moments toward the end of 2004. Since I was a spiritual guy, I kind of said a prayer, something along the lines of *God, what do I do about this woman?*

I heard what I thought was God saying, "Marry her."

That was good enough for me. So I called Erin. We hadn't talked for a couple of weeks since we were in one of those "trough" periods. After catching up, I said, "Look, I really want to try and make this work."

"What does that mean?" Erin asked.

"I don't know. I guess you and me being a full-time couple, sharing this journey through life together."

We batted that idea back and forth, and then I took the plunge. "Will you marry me?" I asked over the phone.

"I don't believe you."

"No, I'm being completely serious. Will you marry me?"

Erin wasn't convinced. But she didn't say no.

The next time I saw her in person, I picked up where I had left off. Inside my apartment, I got down on one knee and officially proposed to her again.

"Show me a ring."

"Okay, I'll buy you a ring."

"I think I want to pick out my own ring."

"We can do that."

That afternoon, we visited the Santa Monica Place shopping mall and found a jewelry store. We looked at rings until she chose one she liked that fit my budget.

Now that she had her engagement diamond, we needed a date. "If you want to take your time, I totally understand," I said.

"No," she said. "I want to be married now."

"Now? As in—"

"Not today, but soon. Very soon."

I let Erin plan everything. She found a minister online—a woman— who was one of those rent-a-reverends. I knew all about mail-order ministers because I had paid $50 to get my State of California license to marry people. I had couples who approached me following one of my lectures at the Philosophical Research Society and asked me, as their learned teacher, if I could marry them. I'd officiated over dozens of marriages over the years.

Erin found a nice venue—a gazebo in a public park in Laguna Beach with a view of the clear blue Pacific. A date was set: Wednesday, December 29—just a month away. We decided to have a very small wedding. Her mother wasn't going to pay for the nuptials anyway, and Erin didn't feel it was fair to ask her grandmother to chip in. (After her grandfather passed away, her grandmother sold their West Hills home and moved to Port Hueneme in Ventura County. Erin was still living with her.)

Thus, we were both interested in a simple, modest wedding. Very simple. We each invited a friend to be our witnesses. Erin asked a girlfriend named Joanna to be her maid of honor, and I asked a good buddy, Jack, to stand in with me. The cost to hold an outdoor wedding in a city park on a Wednesday afternoon in the last week of the year was minimal—free.

On the morning of our big day, dark clouds covered the Southland and rained buckets. At my Santa Monica apartment, I gave her another out. "We can do this another day, if you want."

"Oh, no. We're getting married today," Erin said. If we had to hold umbrellas while we exchanged vows, that's what we were going to do.

In the afternoon, the clouds broke and the sun shone through. The weather was absolutely beautiful in Laguna Beach. We recited our wedding vows overlooking the shimmery Pacific, signed the paperwork, and thanked our two friends for sharing in the moment. Then Erin and I checked into the Surf & Sand Resort, a four-star oceanfront hotel right on Laguna Beach. We stayed there through New Year's Eve and had a wonderful honeymoon.

We settled into married life. Two-and-a-half years later, we were thrilled when Erin learned that she was pregnant. Our son, Dante, was born on February 12, 2008. They say that having a child changes everything about a marriage, and we were no different than any other couple. Erin had her hands full caring for Dante, and I had my hands full at KLOS, working early mornings on the *Mark & Brian Show* and the *Impact* show on Sunday nights. Looking back, I'd say that life was good as we settled into some sort of domestic bliss.

And then my orderly world got tossed upside down.

CURVE BALL

Those working at AM and FM stations have a name for it—"corporate radio."

Radio outlets, at least in the major markets, are big business. Lots of money changes hands. Egos are involved. People are hired and fired. Quickly.

The ABC Network had owned KABC and KLOS since their inceptions in 1925 and 1969, respectively, but during the 2000s, AM and FM stations were buffeted by the winds of change. People didn't need to tune in to a radio station to listen to music or a talk show on their way to work anymore, nor did they need to fuss with the same old CDs. All they had to do was plug in their Apple iPod or mp3 player at work, home, or in the car, and they could listen to the music they wanted. No annoying commercials, either.

Or they could listen to satellite radio. Sirius XM Radio, available by subscription, was making big inroads by offering mostly commercial-free radio stations for every taste in music or talk radio. Satellite radio got a huge boost when the self-described "King of All Media," Howard Stern, took his show to Sirius in 2004.

Nobody was sure if the presence of satellite radio was a good or bad thing for the *Mark & Brian Show*. We figured we were okay. Our Arbitron ratings held steady, longtime advertisers stayed with us, and Mark and Brian were never at a loss to find something funny to say or lampoon famous celebrities.

The winds of change first presented themselves in early 2009. Citadel Broadcasting, the third largest radio station operator in the United States with more than sixty AM stations and 150 FM stations, purchased KABC, KLOS, and the La Cienega property—lock, stock, and barrel, including the radio transmitters.

The rank and file employees had heard stories of new corporate owners coming in and cleaning house, and that's exactly what happened. One of the first to be let go was Rita Wilde, our program director. Twenty-five years at KLOS, helping to brand 95.5 FM as the premier classic rock station in Southern California, didn't save her job. Citadel wanted their own PD at the helm.

A week later, I was called into the office of the new program director. I didn't know what to expect, but after seeing Rita and others get their pink slips, I didn't think I'd be the recipient of any good news.

"Have a seat, Frank," said the PD.

"Sure."

The program director didn't beat around the bush. "Since Citadel took over, we've been taking a fresh look at all the shows on KLOS. The *Impact* show on Sunday nights has nothing to do with the format of this station, so we're taking it off the air."

I was so stunned that I momentarily lost my voice. After gathering my wits, I pleaded my case. "But I've been doing *Impact* for more than twenty-one years. Michael Benner had the show for nine years before me. *Impact* has a long public service tradition at KLOS—"

"We're going in a different direction. The show's over. You're done."

"But what about this Sunday? Surely I can do a farewell show. There has to be some sort of closure."

The program director agreed. Let me tell you, it was an emotional five hours as I announced the end of an era—the final broadcast of *Impact*. I took plenty of calls from fans expressing shock and anger. I did my best to hold my tongue but I couldn't hold back my tears. I wept innumerable times, unable to fully comprehend that it was all over.

Losing *Impact* felt like I had a leg chopped off.

Part of me was missing, for sure. Much of my identity was wrapped up in the *Impact* show, and when that was taken away from me, I was thrown for an emotional loop.

TEEING IT UP

I suddenly had more free time since I didn't have to plan for a five-hour talk show every Sunday night. That was a good news/bad news situation since losing *Impact* also impacted my wallet, but I eventually came to a place where I rolled with it. The new hole in my schedule gave me more time to play golf.

Golf?

I haven't mentioned this before, but I started swinging a club when I was fifteen years old with my best friend, Barry Traub. We'd take our garage sale set of golf clubs over to a pitch-and-putt course in Studio City called Kirkwood Golf (known today as Weddington Golf). I bet we played five times a week that first summer.

Kirkwood was a muni course, your typical nine-hole par-3, a place where kids could learn the game and play for five bucks. I had looped only a handful of rounds when one day, on the ninth hole, I topped a 7-iron. An awful shot. Instead of the ball lofting toward the green, the worm-burner skittered low and rolled and rolled. . . until the ball dropped into the cup for a hole-in-one. After that, I was hooked and played every chance I got.

I put the clubs away for many years following graduation from Notre Dame, but during my *Mark & Brian* years, I picked up the game again. I became a golf nut, so much so that I invited M. Scott Peck, the author of the seminal book, *The Road Less Traveled*, to come on *Impact* and talk about his new book, *Golf and the Spirit: Lessons for the Journey*. His theology placed him clearly in the New Age camp, which made him a perfect guest because he definitely put a metaphysical backspin on life.

"I believe that golf can be a wonderful spiritual path of growth toward God," he stated. I'm not sure I'd go that far since golf can be a pretty frustrating game, but I did feel like I communed with nature when I walked along verdant fairways.

Nine months after I was relieved of my *Impact* host duties in February 2009, I received a text from Tracy Thackrah asking if I would be interested in playing a round of golf sometime soon.

I smiled and thought of the time I first met Tracy. He was an *Impact* fan in his late twenties when he popped up at one of my lectures at the Philosophical Research Society. This would have been around 2004. We hit it off despite a fifteen-year age gap because he was on a search for spirituality and liked everything I had to say about untapping the human potential within us. He bought into humanism and New Age thought in a big way, which is why we became fast friends.

A year after we met, my screener left the show. I asked Tracy if he wanted to help out on Sunday nights. Like my introduction to Michael Benner, Tracy leaped at the chance to work with me and proved to be a quick learner. He developed a knack for finding just the right call at just the right time.

After a couple of years of screening calls on *Impact*, I noticed that Tracy would call in sick from time to time. One particular night, he didn't show up, which meant I had to take unscreened calls on the air. Holy shamoka! In talk radio, that was the equivalent of a high-wire act, picking up calls cold.

I survived, but when I called and asked why he stood me up, Tracy replied that he had to quit his screener job and move to Las Vegas to live with his parents. That sounded like a strange excuse, given his age.

I didn't hear from Tracy for a while. The next time he called, he told me the *real* reason why he had to move to Las Vegas. He confessed that he had an addiction problem with speed—amphetamines that triggered the brain's reward system by giving the user feelings of pleasure.

"But I'm done with speed," Tracy said. "I'm clean now."

"That's great," I replied. I was clean, too. My days of drug use were in my rearview mirror. Hearing about Tracy's change of direction was great news.

"But there's something else," he said.

"What's that?"

"I became a Christian, and I'm going to get baptized at Compass Bible Church in Aliso Viejo this Sunday afternoon. It would mean a lot to me if you came."

"Whoa—wait a minute." Tracy had been one of my disciples. And now he was one of those Jesus Freaks? "What happened?" I asked.

"You know my brother."

"Yeah, I do."

Dale Thackrah was the pastor of biblical care at Compass Bible Church in Orange County. We'd gotten to know each other on the golf course. Even though he was a Christian pastor, I never felt like he was trying to convert me or overload me with Jesus talk. When I was doing the *Impact* show, Dale called in several times *before* Tracy became my screener. I didn't hang up on him because he was careful not to thump the Bible at my audience or me. I can't remember him quoting Scripture on the air, which made him unlike other Christians who phoned the show. He was a thoughtful caller who tried to talk about Jesus without mentioning His name.

After we met, he told me that he was "Dale from Aliso Viejo," which elicited a laugh. He continued to call in after we knew each other, but I didn't let the audience know we were acquainted. He was a golf buddy, a fun-loving guy just like his brother.

When Tracy asked me to attend his baptism, I asked him to explain the change of heart.

"It's like this," he said. "Dale had been witnessing to me for years. When I hit rock bottom, everything he said made sense. You saw how I was—I was going downhill fast. I needed Jesus Christ in my life. When Dale presented the Gospel, I knew it was time. I'm getting baptized, and I'd love for you to be there."

I'm not sure why I said yes, but I did. I hadn't darkened the doorway of a church in decades, except for weddings and the occasional funeral, but there I was at Compass Bible Church when senior pastor Mike Fabarez dunked Tracy. A dozen others were baptized in a public way that Sunday afternoon, cheered on by family and friends. I couldn't help but be struck by the sheer *joy* I saw in everyone's faces.

But that's as far as it went for me. I was a neutral observer, a spiritual man who believed that there were many paths to heaven. Getting baptized and becoming a Christian was just another way.

We were walking back to our cars when Tracy stopped me. "You know, you could become a man of God, too," he said.

Those words hit me hard, even though they shouldn't have. I was pantheistic in my spiritual outlook, meaning I didn't believe in a distinct personal God. I didn't like the exclusivity that Christianity preached. I mumbled something noncommittal and thanked him for his interest in my personal welfare.

Despite our differences in spiritual outlook, I felt comfortable enough with Tracy to rekindle our friendship now that he was back in Orange County. I couldn't help but notice how he was a changed person.

He went from being an erratic personality, nervous and flighty, to a calm, relaxed individual who seemed to be going places in life.

He found a job in radio. He became the assistant program director at KBPK, a low-power FM station operated by the Communications department at Fullerton College, a community college. KBPK, 90.1 FM on the dial, ran an adult contemporary format. I was happy for him and glad he stayed in touch.

Every few months, he texted me a verse from Scripture:

- John 14:6 (ESV): "Jesus said, 'I am the way, and the truth, and the life. No one comes to the Father except through me.'"

- John 3:16 (ESV): "For God so loved the world, that he gave his only son, that whoever believes in him should not perish but have eternal life."

- 2 Corinthians 5:17 (ESV): "Therefore, if anyone is in Christ, he is a new creation. The old has passed away; behold the new has come."

I knew Tracy's intentions were pure; we were too good of friends for me not to think otherwise. But I still had a huge chip on my shoulder regarding Christianity. Too much bad water had passed under the bridge for me to take Jesus Christ—if He existed at all—seriously.

In mid-December 2009, Tracy sent me a text asking if I wanted to play golf with him and his brother. They were living in southern Orange County, while Erin, Dante, and I had moved from West L.A. to Oak Park, near Agoura Hills and Westlake Village in Ventura County.

I gave him a call. "Sure, let's play," I said. "It'll be fun chasing the little white ball."

Tracy suggested playing at the Fullerton Municipal Golf Course— roughly midway between our homes. We looked at our calendars and decided the next Thursday would work.

The date is one that's forever etched in my memory: December 17, 2009.

17

TURN, TURN, TURN

Our tee time was in the early afternoon at Fullerton Municipal. With the shortest day of the year rapidly approaching, I knew we'd have to hurry to get in 18 holes. Plus I had time constraints.

Like most muni courses in Southern California, the groups ahead of us determined our pace of play—and it was slow. We settled into a rhythm, but it soon became apparent that none of us brought our A games that day. We were spraying the ball all over the course.

Then on the third hole, a short par-4, our tee shots found the fairway—a miracle the way we were playing. We were walking to our drives when Dale sidled closer. "Frank, I'm curious about something. What's your biggest hang-up with the Bible?"

His direct question set me on edge, although I didn't give away the unrest I felt inside of me.

I gave his question a few seconds of thought. "I don't know if Jesus is really the Son of God," I responded.

"Hmmm," Dale said. "Interesting."

When Dale didn't follow up with another question, I breathed easier. In fact, Dale didn't say anything more about the Bible or Jesus as we played through. Meanwhile, we continued to hack up the front nine. Our threesome was playing horrible. Chunks, chili dips, and three-putts. At the turn, Tracy suggested that we call it a day and grab something to eat.

"What do you say we go over to Farmer Boys?" he said, referring to a Southern California restaurant chain known for its comfort food fare.

"Great idea," Dale chimed in. "I'm hungry. Plus I've had enough golf to last me a while."

I wasn't having much fun, so I didn't protest.

The nearest Farmer Boys was a few minutes away on Harbor Boulevard. The menu was fairly straightforward: specialty burgers, platter-sized salads, and hefty chicken-and-rice wraps. We settled into a booth and ordered two hamburgers, a patty melt, and fries.

Between bites, I asked Tracy how he was liking KBPK. He said he was glad to be back in radio, but he had something else on his mind.

"Hey, Frank, let's talk about the Ten Commandments, which is God's law that he laid down for Israel."

Here we go again. "What about the Ten Commandments?" I asked.

I knew Tracy wasn't talking about the Cecil B. DeMille movie I saw as a young kid with Charlton Heston in the lead role of Moses. I had a feeling that Tracy wanted to talk about *the* Ten Commandments, which made me uncomfortable.

"Let's walk through some of them," he said. "Have you ever told a lie before?"

I could play this game. "Sure."

"Have you ever stolen anything?"

Inwardly, I winced. I recalled rifling through Dad's safe deposit box and taking an inch-high stack of $20s to the racetrack.

"Yes," I conceded.

"Have you ever committed adultery?"

Tracy had me there. Heather wasn't the only married woman I'd had an affair with. I nodded my head.

"Jesus breaks down the Ten Commandments even more," Tracy continued. "He said if you look upon a woman with lust, then you have committed adultery. Have you ever done that before?"

"Sure. Hasn't everybody?" I wanted to defend myself.

"Have you ever used the Lord's name in vain?"

"Of course." Especially when hanging out at KLOS, where everyone cussed like a sailor on shore leave.

"Let me stop right here," Tracy said. "From what you've said, you're a guilty man in front of God's law. That's bad news, but here's the Good News, Frank. Jesus Christ came on this earth, died on a cross for all of our sins, and fulfilled the righteousness that He demands from us so that we might have eternal life, in heaven, with Him. So Frank, if you repent of your sins and trust in Jesus, you will be found right in the eyes of God."

I nodded. I was listening. But in my mind, I was already right with God because I had been on a spiritual quest since my motorcycle accident. It was all about seeking a higher consciousness.

Then it was Dale's turn. "When I got saved fifteen years ago, it was the best decision I ever made," he said. "Everything changed—my friends, my work, and my outlook. I now have a new perspective because I know I have eternal life. When I said 'yes' to Jesus, I became a new creation, as it says in 2 Corinthians. Better yet, all the guilt I felt for breaking God's laws was completely taken away from me. My old life was gone, and a new life began."

For the next *three* hours, Dale and Tracy tag-teamed me, taking turns explaining the Gospel and hitting me with questions. Dale, with his pastor background, challenged me to defend my New Age beliefs, probing, prodding, and exploring the contours of what I regarded as spiritual truth.

I'll admit that I got defensive. I had never been backed into a corner like this. For someone who had talked about every spiritual approach under the sun for twenty-one years on the radio, as someone who had given hundreds of spiritual lectures over the years, my arguments lacked punch against my friends. If New Age taught that humans were basically good, how did that explain the evil actions of so many? How could men and women be divine if they were liars and cheats, deceitful in every action? History was replete with genocides, oppression, and torture— man's inhumanity against humanity.

Dale and Tracy presented Jesus Christ as the answer to the sins in the world. They reiterated that true morality was revealed by the God of the Bible. Only Scripture contained the message of grace, which was the unmerited favor of God upon His people. Dale reminded me that we had done nothing to deserve His grace, yet He willingly came on this earth to die for our sins so that we could have eternal life with Him.

Dale painstakingly explained who Jesus Christ was—both God and man. Because of the truthfulness of the Bible, I could be confident that He was the Son of God because of what was prophesied hundreds, if not thousands of years earlier in the Old Testament, that he would be born of a virgin, in Bethlehem, in the lineage of David.

Tracy jumped in. Jesus wasn't some impersonal deity, which was the foundation of New Age thought, he said. "The Creator of the Universe wants to have a personal relationship with *you*. How amazing is that?"

The brothers wanted to make sure that I understood what it meant to say yes to Christ. "You can experience the peace that passes all understanding and be assured of having eternal life with Him," Dale said.

What impressed me a great deal about Dale and Tracy was their loving manner. While gentle in spirit, they were resolute in their beliefs. They were doing their best to lay out a case why I should become a believer in Jesus Christ as my Lord and Savior.

Long after our plates had been taken away, Dale leaned in. "Frank, I know you have to go. We've had a great discussion today. You're a Buddhist or whatever, so could you answer me a question before we go? You have a gorgeous wife and year-and-a-half-old son waiting for you. If something happened to you on the freeway and you didn't make it back home, would you be right with God?"

"Yeah, I would be," I replied without hesitation. "What kind of question is that? I'm a spiritual person. Of course I'm right with God."

Dale smiled. "Would you do me a favor? Would you meditate on that question before you turn on the ignition and leave?"

I noticed that Dale used the word *meditate*. He didn't say *pray*. He was speaking the language I knew.

"Sure."

"Good, because before you put the key in the ignition, I don't want you to drive home without thinking about what we're talking about, which is that Jesus Christ is the Son of God. If He is the Son of God, that changes everything about how we understand reality to be. Jesus Christ is real. I love you, brother, but if you get in your car and get hit by a bus and die, you're going to go to hell. I don't want that to happen. Please consider what we've said today, and meditate upon the things that we're talking about."

"I promise you that I will." But even after three hours of deep discussion with Dale and Tracy, I didn't see how this was going to change things or do me any good.

When we departed Farmer Boys, it was already dark outside. Despite their boldness, despite their directness, I knew Dale and Tracy had my back. If anything, I was cognizant these guys cared deeply for me. They really wanted the best for me.

I watched Tracy hop into Dale's truck, and they took off. I opened my car door and sat behind the wheel. Dale said to meditate, right? So I settled myself. Closed my eyes. Took a series of deep breaths. This exercise of calming myself was something I had learned from Eckhart Tolle, a German-born author and speaker thought to be one of the most spiritually influential persons in the world. Oprah loved him and had him on her show frequently. Tolle was a quote machine about New Age spirituality, saying things like "The past has no power over the present moment," or "The primary cause of unhappiness is never the situation but your thoughts about it."

Instead of being impressed as I sat in my car, his sayings sounded like hogwash. They were platitudes that really didn't amount to a hill of beans. Tolle's teachings did nothing to calm my mind. Instead of settling into a meditative state, the opposite happened. I felt agitated. I started heating up. My chest became really hot. The sensation of warmth over-taking my respiratory system overwhelmed me.

The intense heat inside my chest kept rising. I felt *hot*. I had never experienced anything like this before, not even when I was down with a really high fever.

I did a mental check . . . and thought about what Dale said. Was I right with God? I was honest with myself, and the answer unsettled me. I didn't know for sure.

And then I heard a distinct voice in the middle of my brain:

Are you ready to submit to Me?

The utterance was so clear in my mind that I knew instantly the Lord of Lords, the Creator of the universe, the ruler of all things—Jesus Christ—was speaking into my heart. Don't ask me how, but I *knew*.

He was the Alpha and the Omega, the beginning and the end. My heart told me I needn't look any further than Jesus. All the New Age stuff I had believed for decades tumbled like a house of cards. My search was over . . . if I submitted to His will.

Although I felt weird about what was happening to me—the heat in my chest, the swirling thoughts in my mind—I didn't feel coerced. I had a choice to make. Life wasn't falling apart. I had a beautiful wife and a child. A nice place to live. I was gainfully employed. Successful by the world's standards. Sure, I had lost the *Impact* show a few months earlier, but I was still alive and kicking. There was plenty of gas left in the tank.

Yet I was being asked by this Voice—the one I recognized as the Lord

Jesus Christ—to submit to Him and let Him lead my life. This was a Voice that could not be denied. My search for spirituality was over.

I bowed my head. "Yes, Lord, I will submit to You," I whispered.

And then He said words that would change the direction of my life.

Then pick up your cross and follow Me.

I couldn't ignore this imperative either. "Yes, Lord. I will," I whispered again.

I had no idea what I was supposed to do next. I sat in my car a little longer. I didn't hear anything more from the Voice, but I knew I had given my life to Jesus Christ.

My body began to cool down. I had to tell Tracy or Dale what happened. I pulled out my cell phone and called Tracy since he wasn't driving.

On the 57 freeway, going south, Tracy heard his ringtone and looked at the number. "Hey, Frank's calling," he said to his brother.

He took the call. "Frank, good to hear from you."

"You're not going to believe what happened," I said.

"What?"

"I just gave my life to Christ."

"Praise God! Hallelujah, brother! Wait, you have to share this with Dale."

I heard some fumbling, then Dale's voice. "Frank, don't tell me—"

"It's true. I was sitting in my car, thinking about what you said, when I heard the Lord say, 'Will you submit to Me?' I said, 'Yes, I will.'"

"Praise the mighty name of Jesus!" Dale cried out.

I heard the two brothers hooting and hollering with excitement, punctuating the air with shouts of "Praise God!" and "Hallelujah!"

There was a lot of excitement in the air, and they said they'd be in touch later. I reached down and turned the ignition.

In many ways, I was fired up to see what happened next.

SOCIAL MEDIA

After Tracy was dropped off, the first thing he did was go to his home computer and log on to his Facebook account. He tapped in the following post:

A good friend just gave his life to Christ.

That's all Tracy wrote.

I had a much longer drive to Oak Park. When I got home, Erin was sitting in the living room. I was glad to see her, especially because I had this great news to—

Erin looked at me. "Don't tell me you gave your life to Christ."

"Yeah, I did. Wait—how did you know?"

"I saw it on Tracy's Facebook page."

Erin, like many of her generation, spent a lot of time on Facebook and was friends with my friends. Even though Tracy didn't mention me by name, Erin knew who I was playing golf with that afternoon.

"But—"

"Don't talk to me. I don't want to hear about it."

"Erin, listen—"

"Don't talk to me."

She was really angry. This news blew up her world. As far as she was concerned, her husband had jumped off a high diving board—and into a drained pool.

I was bummed that Erin didn't take the news well. I tried to describe my momentous afternoon with Tracy and Dale, what led me to making a decision for Christ—but she didn't want hear of it. When she busied herself in the kitchen and avoided eye contact, I got the message.

Erin was royally ticked in ways I hadn't seen before. I sent Dale a text and asked him to pray for me, telling him that Erin had found out that I had become a Christian and wasn't happy.

That night, I can't remember if I was banished to the couch, but I know we weren't lovey-dovey. In the early morning hours, a Friday, I drove to the KLOS studios in a distraught state. I was still worked up emotionally about my conversion experience and wondered if I'd be able to perform my engineering job on the *Mark & Brian Show*.

In the predawn darkness, I found an empty office and fell to the floor on my knees. I lowered my head and prayed, "Lord, please help me. Lord, I need Your help." Tears flowed down my cheeks from the raw emotion.

I heard footsteps and looked up. A white man in his late sixties stood in the doorway. I recognized him. He was Lynn Mink, the janitor during the early morning hours.

"Are you okay, Frank?" he asked. Lynn spoke with a syrupy Southern drawl. I didn't know him well, but he always struck me as a sweet, gentle man.

"No," I replied. In the past, I would have said I was doing fine, but after giving my life to Christ, it was time to strip all the pretense away. I decided to tell him exactly what happened the day before and how I said yes to Jesus. But I also made myself vulnerable by including my wife's outraged reaction.

Lynn listened and didn't interrupt. When I finished, he said, "Do you want me to pray with you?"

I couldn't pass on that. "Yeah, sure. Are you a Christian?"

"Well, I'm a pastor."

Wasn't that just so God? In my time of need, He sent a janitor/pastor to minister to me at a time when I needed prayer. That pre-dawn encounter started a regular routine in which Lynn and I would regularly meet for prayer before *Mark & Brian* came on the air.

Dale called me later that day to follow up with me. We talked about how perturbed Erin was. He counseled me to continue loving her, treating her special. She needed to see how *I* had changed.

Then Dale had a question. "Do you have a Bible?" he asked. Before I could reply, he said, "Of course, you don't own a Bible. You hated Christians. I'm going to mail you one. What's your address?"

I gave my street address, and Dale said he'd go on Amazon and drop-ship me an *ESV Study Bible*.

"Thank you. That would be nice."

The *ESV Study Bible*, using the English Standard Version translation, arrived in the mail from Amazon a good week later. I didn't open it right away. Late one night, I couldn't sleep, so I picked up the Bible and flipped to a random page. I looked down, and Luke 9:23 jumped out at me like the passage was written in orange neon: "And he said to all, 'If anyone would come after me, let him deny himself and take up his cross daily and follow me.'"

Whoa. That passage of Scripture hit me like a blow to the solar plexus. The Lord had said the same thing to me in the Farmer Boys parking lot.

I got on my knees. *Lord, I will follow You. I don't know what that means, but I will follow You in obedience.*

It was time to take up my cross.

SUNDAY MORNINGS

One thing Tracy talked to me about was finding me a good church. He stressed the important of plugging into a solid, Bible-believing congregation and being fed nutritious spiritual food from the pulpit.

"Grace Community is driving distance from your home. John MacArthur is the pastor there. He's one of the biggest pillars in the Christian faith."

I visited Grace Community Church the following Sunday, but I didn't have a good experience. John MacArthur was in the pulpit that morning, but the church was too button-down and traditional for this former rock 'n' roll guy.

I happened to be speaking with Dale when I told him I wasn't a good match for Grace Community. Did he know of a church that would be a better fit?

"Try Cornerstone in Simi Valley," Dale said. "The pastor is an Asian-American with a shaved head and a cool-looking goatee. Name is Francis Chan."

I walked into Cornerstone while the worship band was playing an emotional number. I spotted Francis Chan in the front row. He was lifting his arms in praise and totally into his act of adoration for the Lord of the Universe. It didn't take long for my heart to melt. Within minutes, I was on my knees, crying and thanking the Lord for loving a sinner like me. Francis Chan's sermon blew me away. It was like he was speaking to *me*.

I had found a church home.

ALL IN

Dale and Tracy followed up with me often. They recommended that I read three books: *The Case for Christ* by Lee Strobel, *Mere Christianity* by C.S. Lewis, and *More than a Carpenter* by Josh McDowell.

I spent three months reading the trio of books. My goal was to go from believing to knowing. When I was a New Age believer, I framed Jesus as one of the great spiritual teachers. But that's not who He was. I read *More than a Carpenter*, followed by *The Case for Christ*, which pretty much sealed the deal for me. By the time I got to *Mere Christianity*, I was particularly struck by C.S. Lewis' contention that Jesus was either a liar, a lunatic, or Lord. He had to be one of the three, and He wasn't a liar or a lunatic. That's when I fully said in my mind, *There's no doubt that Jesus is Lord.*

On the home front, Erin was doubting my sanity. We had many interesting discussions the first few weeks. She saw me reading my *ESV Study Bible*. She saw me going to Cornerstone, week after week. She saw that this Jesus thing was real, not a passing fad.

A couple of months after my conversion experience, she told me that I had to make a choice: either her or Christ.

"I'm sorry, honey, it will always be Him first. But you're right after Him, and He commands me to love you as He loves the church."

Meanwhile, I read my *ESV Study Bible* ravenously.

I stopped doing public lectures at the Philosophical Research Society. I made an announcement on my website that I had become a Christian and was following a new path. I received a ton of mean-spirited postings, but I shrugged my shoulders.

Pick up your cross . . .

Late in February, I read in the bulletin that Cornerstone would be holding a baptism on Sunday, March 7, 2010. I called Dale and asked him if he thought I was ready.

"Sure, you are," he replied. "That's really great that you want to get baptized."

Now let me share with you what Dale had to say about the experience:

> **Dale Thackrah:** When Frank told me that he was thinking about getting baptized, I was living in Arizona. Since our golf outing, I had taken a new job as the pastor of care and biblical counseling at Redemption Gateway Church in Mesa, Arizona, around twenty miles southeast of Phoenix.
>
> I woke on Saturday morning, the day before the baptism, and said to my wife, Shawna, "Let's go to California. I don't want to miss Frank's baptism."
>
> I have an awesome wife, so she was up for it. We drove to her parents' home in Orange County and spent Saturday night there. Then we got up early Sunday morning for the ninety-minute drive to Cornerstone.
>
> I knew Tracy was going to be there, too, but I didn't know that he would share Frank's coming-to-Christ story with one of the pastors before the service started. Next thing I knew, that pastor tapped me on the shoulder and asked if I wanted to baptize Frank.
>
> Would I? I didn't have to be asked twice.
>
> What an honor to stand in the baptismal pool and ask Frank if he believed that Jesus Christ died for his sins so that he could have eternal life with Him. He said yes.
>
> "Based upon your profession of faith in the Lord Jesus Christ, I now baptize you in the name of the Father,

the Son, and the Holy Spirit," I said. And then I dunked him.

What an amazing moment for the both of us. You see, I grew up in Southern California and had been listening to Frank on the radio for many years. There was a time in my life, before I got saved at the age of twenty-seven, that I actually agreed with a lot of what Frank was saying on KLOS. But that all changed when I gave my life to Christ.

Then my brother, Tracy, became a good friend and started working for Frank as his screener. I can remember a lot of nights, praying in desperation to the Lord, asking Him to help with Tracy's drug problem and knowing the New Age philosophy that Frank was ingraining into him was not good for my brother's spiritual health. I really struggled with that. I thought about trying to torpedo their relationship and really blow Frank out of the water because I knew Tracy was being influenced by Frank in a negative way.

If it was up to me and my flesh, I would have done something to break up their friendship, but God put it on my heart to pray for the both of them instead. That's what I did.

I remember Tracy telling me stories about what he was learning about the New Age movement. I continued to pray for him and challenge him in his thinking. Then, when he hit rock bottom, I had the unbelievable experience of sharing the Gospel with Tracy and praying with him the night he got saved in 2006.

Tracy grew in his faith. We were both concerned about Frank and prayed for an opportunity to share Christ with him. It was Tracy's idea to ask Frank to play golf with us on December 17, 2009. Frank didn't know this, but we had an agenda that day. We had every intention of using this golf outing as an opportunity to share the Gospel with Frank.

I had a forty-mile drive to Fullerton Municipal Golf Course. That day, I remember praying the entire time that God would give me the wisdom and the necessary words for Frank to understand the Gospel.

When I asked him if he was right with God if something happened to him on the freeway, he was bothered by my question. Frank is the kind of guy who would never let you know he was bothered. But I could tell through his body language and the way he continued to talk to me that he was getting challenged in a way that wasn't comfortable for him.

Honestly, Frank is an intellectual, and he is used to controlling and directing the conversation. There was a real sense, sitting in a booth at Farmer Boys, that Frank wasn't in control. I remember praying, as I was talking to him, *God, please show him who is in control. Show Frank that it's not him but You.*

Here's how our conversation went:

Dale: Frank, do you believe in absolute truth?

Frank: You can't say anything is absolutely true today. Truth is relative to one's own circumstances.

Dale: Don't you really mean that circumstances are evidence of truth? Meaning, aren't they really just evidence of the reality of moral or universal truth?

Frank: No, I believe what's true for you may not be true for me.

Dale: If it was my "truth" that we should kill anyone who ever stole a car, would you be okay with that?

Frank: No.

Dale: Why?

Frank: We have laws against stealing cars.

Dale: I don't like those laws. I think those laws are subjective. They aren't true for me.

Frank: You're being ridiculous.

Dale: No. I am expressing what I believe. Who are you to judge my truth? So let me ask you this: Instead of stealing your car, can I have your car?

Frank: Huh? What do you mean?

Dale: If I picked up the keys to your car and drove off, and you never saw me again . . . would you call the police and turn me in for stealing your car?

Frank: Um . . . yeah. I guess I would.

Dale: Why?

Frank: Because it's my car.

Dale: But I want it. I've determined that your car is now mine because I need transportation. That's my truth.

Frank: We have laws that we all have to follow for the good of society.

Dale: You've expressed a truth. Is your expressed moralism subject to an outside force?

Frank: Yes, sure it is. Society has determined that these rules matter.

Dale: Frank, are you sure that society determined these truths, or rules against stealing cars, or was it something that our Creator instilled in us? It seems that you are confusing preference with truth.

Frank: What do you mean?

Dale: I'm arguing that relativism is a fraud. I believe there is a universal truth and a universal truth determiner—and He calls Himself God. You and I don't get to define what truth is because He is the One who has already done that. He says that about Himself . . . that He is Truth in John 14:6. That's a truth claim that is either true or false.

You've already said that you think Jesus was a good man. That He was one of the best teachers who ever lived. That if the world followed the teachings of Christ, we would be much better off, right?

Frank: Yes.

Dale: But if you read John 14:6 and other Scriptures where He proclaims that God is Truth and that He is God . . . and you reject that, then you can't say Jesus was a good man and a good teacher because that would make him a horrible, wicked liar. Jesus would just be another religious con man, if you will. You can't have it both ways.

Either what He said is true—and has eternal ramifications—or He is a liar and all of His teaching should be rejected. Do I have that right?

Frank: (after a long silence) Let me think about that.

You could tell that he was really struggling with not having snappy answers. His New Age philosophy really painted him into a corner. What I was trying to do was get him to the place where he had to give a defense for his theology, which he couldn't do. Then I presented the Gospel to him and explained why Jesus Christ was the better and real solution to the issues he was dealing with.

When I called him the following day, after he told Tracy and me that he had given his life to Christ, I made sure that Frank understood what the Gospel was all about. By the time we hung up, it became very clear to me that he had repented of his sins and accepted the forgiveness of the Savior. As a pastor, sometimes I'm guilty of wanting to get all the details, but the Spirit doesn't always work that way. My time on the phone proved that Frank was born again, for sure.

When Frank was on the *Impact* show, he was an apologist for the New Age movement. He defended a belief system that was warped and had many dead ends and potholes. I was confident that once he knew the Truth, and the Truth got a hold of him, then he would become a tremendous apologist for Jesus.

What happened on December 17, 2009, was an amazing moment in time. All the credit and glory goes to God. Tracy and I were just instruments in the Redeemer's hands.

Can you believe what Dale and Tracy did for me—the boldness in their mission?

What happened on that December day set into motion a series of events that defy belief.

18

KNOCKING ON
HEAVEN'S DOOR

A month after I got baptized, Francis Chan stunned the thousands who called Cornerstone home with an announcement that he was stepping away from the church he had founded sixteen years earlier. Francis, who'd written a mega-selling book, *Crazy Love*, said he felt God was calling him to resign even though he wasn't sure what the Lord was calling him to do next.

Pastor Chan's announcement threw me for a loop. I felt like I had lost my rock in the pulpit. I'm sure I wasn't the only person to feel that way.

I didn't feel as connected with the new preacher taking over for Francis. I church-shopped, but without mooring to a particular church, I felt like I was cast adrift. Sometimes I didn't go to church for two or three weeks at a time. It wasn't like I had lost any of my newfound faith, but I just didn't feel linked to a church body.

There was another issue in play: my marriage. Since Erin and I weren't on the same page spiritually, this created a new dynamic in our relationship. Speaking bluntly, we were unequally yoked. It wasn't her fault. She married me when we both had the same belief system. We wanted to be spiritual, not religious. But then I came home from the golf outing and professed to be a Christian. I said I heard Christ talking to me. She probably thought I had lost my mind.

In order to gain my bearings, I spent a lot of time reading and re-reading 1 Corinthians 7:12-16 (ESV):

> To the rest I say (I, not the Lord) that if any brother has a wife who is an unbeliever, and she consents to live with him, he should not divorce her. If any woman has a husband who is an unbeliever, and he consents to live with her, she should not divorce him. For the unbelieving husband is made holy because of his wife, and the unbelieving wife is made holy because of her husband. Otherwise your children would be unclean, but as it is, they are holy.
>
> But if the unbelieving partner separates, let it be so. In such cases the brother or sister is not enslaved. God has called you to peace. For how do you know, wife, whether you will save your husband? Or how do you know, husband, whether you will save your wife?

Scripture was quite clear: if Erin consented to live with me, I was not to divorce her. But if she made the separation from me, the ball was in her court.

During the summer of 2010, nine months after my conversion experience, our marriage was on tenterhooks. The state of the union was hanging by a thread. I heard a preacher on the radio say that in a marriage like mine, there was an 80 percent chance that the other spouse would never come to Christ.

Too much drama was going on between us. Erin had arrived at her wit's end. In her mind, I was *not* the guy she married. She had chosen as her life partner a spiritual man who sought the wisdom of the ages, not someone who pored over the study notes at the bottom of each page in his Bible.

I suggested counseling. She said fine, but no Christian counselors. Based on the way the wind was blowing, I figured any sort of conversation with a neutral third party in the room couldn't hurt. We met with a secular counselor who had a New Age outlook on things, and from the first session, I felt like we were going in circles.

On Monday, September 27, 2010, I was at Fairplex Park, a racetrack at the Pomona Fairgrounds. My love for horses was still as strong as ever. In fact, I was there to watch *my* horse—a thoroughbred named Foolin' that I owned. Yes, I was a race horse owner, which was a long story in itself. (Trust me, the investment was modest.)

I was standing on the top row of the grandstand, hanging out between races, when Erin called my cell. She was in Seattle visiting her family.

"I don't know how to say this, so I'll just say it," she began. "This marriage is not working. I want out."

"Wait—Erin. Let's keep trying."

"No, I want a divorce. It'll be better for the both of us."

"What about Dante?"

"I'm done."

When the sad phone call was over, I put my smartphone back in my pocket and looked over the grandstand railing. The distance to the ground had to be a good five or six stories. That was high enough to end things. All I had to do was hop the railing, and my troubles would be over.

For twenty seconds, I had a conversation with myself about whether I should jump. And then the reality of what that action would mean hit me in the chest: *You have a young son. You can't leave him. Your troubles would be over, but what about Erin and Dante, who'd be left behind?*

I didn't jump. I decided that I hadn't come this far—making a decision for Christ—only to lose my family. I was hoping that at some level, we could pull from the same rope and make this marriage work. For us. For our son.

I sought counsel from one of the elders at Cornerstone. His take: *Tell her you love her. Remind her of that as much as you can. God has a plan, but in the meantime, you gotta take it. You're gonna suffer a lot. Welcome to the role of a Christian.*

Okay, I had to suck it up, so that's what I did. Each day was a test, but I was determined to hang in there.

When Erin called the following day, she had calmed down and come to the point where she said, "You know, we have a son. I want to try and make it work. I still hate you, but I can hang in there a little longer."

In my mind, that was a partial victory. I'd take it.

I picked them up at the train station the following evening, determined to simply love on her. "God's in my life, and I know He wants us to be together," I told her.

And that's all I did. I stuck a smile on my face. I was cheerful. Helpful around the house. Put dishes in the dishwasher. Ran errands without being asked to. Played with Dante to give her a break. Treated her nice.

Over the next few months, like a thaw in U.S.-Soviet relations, we reached a détente. We were okay with each other. We even had our tender moments. I could tell she was watching me. Was I a new person—meaning was I truly loving and honoring her—now that I identified myself as a Christian? That became my guiding credo.

In early 2011, I still wasn't tethered to a particular church. Then I remembered a pastor that Francis Chan spoke highly of: Britt Merrick, who shepherded a church named Reality in Carpinteria, south of Santa Barbara.

Suntanned, fortyish, with sun-bleached blond hair and looking like he stepped out of a Beach Boys album cover from the early '60s, Britt Merrick checked all the boxes for me. We were living in Westlake at the time, just west of the San Fernando Valley, so Reality Carp—as locals called it—wasn't too far, but it was still a good forty-five minute drive. I didn't mind commuting to church if I got spiritually fed. Britt Merrick proved to be a great Bible teacher.

I would come home early Sunday afternoon, and Erin would ask me questions. I could tell she was somewhat interested in what I was doing. Then one Sunday morning in April, I was getting dressed to go to Reality Carp when Erin stepped into our bedroom. "I want to go to church with you," she said.

Wow. A crack in the door. I didn't know what prompted the change in heart, but I wasn't going to probe. "That would be wonderful, honey."

It was awfully quiet in the car the entire way there. I know I was trying to control my thoughts—and not get too ahead of myself. At the same time, though, I couldn't deny that this could be big.

When we arrived at Reality Carp, I tried to not be a mother hen. No hovering, no monitoring. I just worshipped God and honored Him.

When we got back in the car, we drove along the coast on the 101. Erin turned her gaze from the blue Pacific and spoke to me. "I really liked that church. People were nice. I don't buy into the Jesus thing, but that was really different than the church I used to go to growing up."

She didn't want to accompany me to Reality Carp the following Sunday, however. That was fine with me. She was free to come and go as she pleased—hands off the wheel. But then she accompanied me to church on a fairly consistent basis, probably three out of four weekends a month. All this time, I don't remember having any deep conversations about Jesus. I kept reminding myself of the words one of the pastors said to me: "Keep your emotions throttled. Just love her as best as you can—as Christ loved the church. Don't think about your own stuff. You need to show her Christ-like love because she's obviously never seen it."

On Sunday, July 3, 2011, an assistant pastor filled in for Britt Merrick. During his message, the assistant pastor said something that really hit Erin hard. I could tell out of the corner of my eye that she was brushing away tears. Again, though, I gave Erin her space.

The worship band came back to play several songs before the end of the service. She leaned over with damp eyes. "I think I need to go up and pray with him."

I remember saying, "Well, go!"

I watched her go forward. The assistant pastor hadn't done an altar call, but he did say that if anyone needed prayer, he and some of the elders were available.

I sat down and bowed my head, trying not to look. But I had to peek. I saw the assistant pastor place his right arm on her left shoulder. Both heads were bowed. He was praying on her.

Erin stayed with him for several minutes, and then she returned to her seat, eyes downcast because she didn't want me to see her crying. I know my wife.

When the service was over, we walked to the car, not saying a thing. Ten minutes into the drive, Erin blurted, "I think I just gave my life to Christ."

I nearly steered the car off the 101. "That's nice," I said, trying to act calm and block out my emotions. But deep inside, I was screaming and rejoicing.

Erin became very animated after this day about Christ. I remember giving her a Bible, which she couldn't put down. She seemed to be in a hurry to learn all she could about what it meant to have a personal relationship with Jesus Christ. She also wanted to get baptized right away. Two weeks after she said yes to Jesus, she was baptized at Carpinteria State Beach, just steps from the church campus. She reminded me that this was the beach her grandparents would take her to when she was a young girl. "God brought me back here," she said.

I was so grateful that we could walk with the Lord together. We immediately changed the way we were raising our little boy. At night-time, after reading him a Bible story, we would ask him if he was ready to pray to Jesus. He was right there, holding our hands and praying. At the end, when I said, "In Jesus' name," our beautiful three-year-old said, "Amen."

We weren't out of the woods yet, but we saw a sustainable path to moving forward together.

POSTING ON YOUTUBE

Something else happened during the summer of 2011. A dear friend of mine, Craig Parker Adams, said I should put something up on YouTube about what happened in my life. Craig knew my whole story.

"A lot of people we know want to know what happened to you," he said. "After *Impact* went off the air, you just kind of dropped out. What about making a video of your testimony?"

I thought for a moment. "Sure, I like your idea. What do we do next?"

Craig ran a recording studio in Hollywood. He was a sound guy and a musician. Incredible guitarist. "I can record you and get it posted," he said.

I drove to Craig's studio and sat at a table with a simple background of stained plywood. I looked at him—Craig was off-camera—and shared my story of redemption in two twelve-minute videos.

The format was loose and impromptu—just a conversation between two friends, but with a bigger goal in mind: sharing the Gospel. Craig posted both videos on YouTube, and it wasn't long before I had hundreds of hits.

One of those who saw my YouTube testimony knew just the person to share it with.

19

ALL ALONG THE
WATCHTOWER

As I grew in my walk with Christ, I regularly listened to a Christian
radio station in Los Angeles with the call letters KKLA. I loved the
great preaching and great teaching whenever I tuned in to 99.5 FM on
the dial. Most of the daytime programming was repackaged sermons
from notables like John MacArthur, Greg Laurie, and Chuck Swindoll.
I also enjoyed the half-hour sermonettes from pastors JP Jones of Cross-
line Community Church in Laguna Hills and Philip De Courcy of
Kindred Community Church in Anaheim Hills.

After twelve-and-a-half hours of preaching and ministry programs
that started at 3:30 a.m., a radio host named Frank Pastore changed up
the programming mix by presenting a live talk show from 4 to 7 p.m.
weekdays. His three-hour broadcast was similar to what I did at *Impact*—
topical monologues, interviews with guests, calls from listeners—but
was different in one all-important area: there was no search for spirituality on the *Frank Pastore Show*. Jesus Christ was the way, the truth, and
the life. Game over.

On March 30, 2012, a listener named James Grainger sent an email to
the show's Facebook page. James was an acquaintance of Frank because
they attended the same church, Calvary Chapel Chino Valley. James

also happened to work for Nestlé USA in a high-rise building that was a stone's throw from the KKLA studios in the California Credit Union Building in Glendale. Despite their proximity to each other at church and work, James and Frank didn't know each other well, but James, a KLOS listener, knew I had become a Christian because Mark and Brian occasionally teased me about it on the air.

James wrote this posting on the Frank Pastore Facebook page: "The question was asked about who we would like to hear interviewed. I have a thought. He is Frank Sontag, and he works at KLOS on the *Mark & Brian Show* here in Los Angeles. I think he has a great testimony of where he came from and how he came to Christ. I think it would be interesting to hear how he handles being a Christian and working in the environment that he does—a rock station on a typical morning show." James included links to the pair of YouTube videos in which I shared the story of my conversion.

To Frank Pastore, this was a fish-out-of-water story. Here was some dude—he loved calling guests on his show "dude"—working at the biggest rock 'n' roll station in L.A. and having a conversion experience. On top of that, he announced his change in heart to the world on YouTube!

Frank checked me out. Googled me. Made phone calls. Asked questions. Looked at my YouTube videos. Satisfied that my story was legit, he reached out to me and asked if I would be interested in coming on his show and sharing my testimony.

"Would I? I'd be thrilled to come on KKLA," I said. We looked at dates and came up with April 25, 2012, a Wednesday.

Now it was my turn to do some research on Frank Pastore. I had heard his show a couple of times when I was doing *Impact*—I liked keeping tabs on other talk show hosts in L.A.—and thought he was really pompous. Didn't like him. But after coming to Christ, I gave him another listen and thought, *This guy is incredible*. I fell in love with Frank, in terms of his persona.

He, too, had an interesting coming-to-Jesus story. Like me, Frank Pastore—pronounced *Pas-tore-ee*—had grown up in an Italian-Catholic family. His hometown was Alhambra, a San Gabriel Valley suburb eight miles southeast of downtown Los Angeles. Waves of Italian immigrants settled in Alhambra in the 1950s, much like the Italian families who found a home in Collinwood, my old Cleveland neighborhood. Frank was two years younger than me, born on August 21, 1957. He also grew up in a dysfunctional family situation. His parents never showed emotion, never kissed on the lips, and never slept in the same bedroom.

Frank attended an all-boys Catholic high school, similar to me. While I graduated from Notre Dame in Sherman Oaks with a less-than-stellar GPA, Frank was the class valedictorian at Damien High in La Verne, Class of '75. He outclassed me in sports as well. Frank was a star pitcher in high school, one of the best in Southern California.

He signed with the Cincinnati Reds out of high school and made it to the major leagues in 1979. He stuck with the big club and moved into the full-time rotation the following season. He married his childhood sweetheart, Gina, and they became parents of two kids, Frank, Jr. and Christina.

Frank was rolling along, putting together a nice Major League career, when everything changed in an instant. While pitching before friends and family in Dodger Stadium, second baseman Steve Sax smashed a wicked line drive through the box. The ball careened off Frank's elbow on his pitching arm, shattering bone. In the midst of excruciating pain, he could feel bits of elbow moving around, much like bits of Oreos in a baggy.

Frank was an atheist when his life crumbled around him. He had walked—no, run away—from the Catholic faith after he accepted his high school diploma. Again, the parallels to my story amazed me.

After getting nailed on the mound, Frank had to be taken out of the game. Several of Frank's teammates—all Christians—found him getting treatment in the clubhouse after the game. When they said they wanted to pray for him, Frank rolled his eyes. Their request made him feel like he had been cast in a cheesy Hallmark movie. He didn't believe in that Jesus stuff. God didn't exist. Life was one hassle after another, and then you die.

One of his teammates asked Frank to come to their Bible study back in Cincinnati, led by a pastor. In a moment of weakness, he said yes, but with his right arm in a sling, Frank showed up determined to launch on those guys. He told his teammates that he wanted to know what was true in life, but the Bible wasn't historical, wasn't accurate, and that the documents and transcripts had been corrupted over the centuries. He blasted the entire premise of the truth of Scripture.

"Finished?" asked the pastor leading the study.

"Yeah."

"You know, you said a lot of things," the pastor said, "but I don't have any answers for you. You said one thing that stuck out to me, though, and it's that you want to believe what's true and what's real. Frank, I want to believe what's true and what's real, so will you help me?"

Frank's teammates looked at each other. Had their pastor flipped out and gone over to the dark side? The pastor, it turned out, knew exactly what he was doing. He told Frank that he had brought two books with him—C.S. Lewis' *Mere Christianity* and *Evidence that Demands a Verdict* by Josh McDowell—and suggested that Frank read both books and share what he learned at their next meeting. If the authors confirmed in his mind that God was not real, that would be okay. "Then I can become happy and fulfilled like you," the pastor said.

Hearing this story about Frank blew my mind. Those were the same authors I had read when I was trying to decide whether Jesus Christ was who He said He was!

Like Frank, my world was upended when I read C.S. Lewis and Josh McDowell's explanations of what Christianity was all about. In Frank's case, after a time of reflection, Frank made the decision to believe that Jesus Christ—the Son of God—had come on this earth to die for our sins and give us a path to the Father in heaven.

Frank said he was clearing out the entire five o'clock hour for me. So it was with great anticipation and joy that I drove to the KKLA office building on that April afternoon after wrapping up at KLOS.

I immediately liked Frank from the first bear hug. A shiny, clean-shaven head framed his cherubic, soft face. His round eyes were warm and inviting. Although he was beefy and no longer at his playing weight—he'd wolfed down a 72-ounce rib-eye steak and all the trimmings in nine minutes, thirty seconds at a Texas restaurant one time on a dare—he wasn't out of shape.

This is how our time unfolded on April 25, 2012:

> **Frank Pastore:** (talking over the lead-in music) 99.5 FM, KKLA Los Angeles. The intersection of faith and reason right here on the *Frank Pastore Show*. Hee-ha and welcome aboard.
>
> Get this now. You guys, I've shared my testimony several times on the air. Briefly, I'm a major league base-ball player with the Cincinnati Reds. Forced to hang out with the Christians on the Reds because if my wife found out that I was going out and clubbing with the

non-Christians, she was going to go home. Leave me. A long story.

A pitch is thrown in Dodger Stadium. The batter swings, and the ball crashes off my elbow. My world is rocked. These Christians I'm hanging out with invite me to a Bible study. Of course, I don't want to go, but I go. I'm challenged to simply disprove Christianity. I was asked to read two Christian books—I didn't even know Christians wrote books. I thought they were all stupid. But I read C.S. Lewis' *Mere Christianity* and *Evidence that Demands a Verdict* by Josh McDowell.

I got to that 50.1 percent place where you go, "You know, I don't have all the answers yet, but I've got enough answered." I'm at that tipping point, right? I chose to become a Christian.

I don't want to offend people, but there is something about Christians who come to Christ in adulthood. There's a flame that burns hotter, brighter, and more distinctly than those who always grew up in the church.

The way it should work is this way: *Everyone should grow up in a Christian family.* That's the ideal, right? Let's not sensationalize and make heroes of the heroin drug dealer who comes to Christ. No, the goal for our children is for them to say, *You know, I never knew a time when I wasn't a Christian.* That's the goal.

Nevertheless, there's something about hearing from people who come to Christ late in life and their perspective on things. For me, I never signed up for "Churchianity." When I came to Christ and self-identified as a Christian, I didn't have a fish on the car or a leather Bible or know who Petra was or Sandy Patti or Stryper or Amy Grant. I didn't have the lingo down.

My guest, Frank Sontag, is not a new name in radio. In fact, he has been in radio for more than thirty years now. If you listen to 95.5 KLOS, then you know of the *Mark & Brian Show* and Frank Sontag. Maybe you've seen his testimony on YouTube.

Frank grew up in Cleveland, playing the accordion in an Italian-Catholic family. He moved with his family to L.A. in the mid-1960s when he was ten years old. He went to Catholic schools and probably had the nuns beating him over the knuckles with a ruler, just like me.

Upon hearing Frank say that, my first thought was this: *How did he know about Sister Patrick Marie?*

Frank Pastore: But get this. In 1984, he got into a motor-cycle accident that rocked his world and sent him on a search for God and significance and meaning that ulti-mately culminated in him coming to Christ just a few years ago in 2009.

I've invited him on the show to share his testimony because I got an email from Jim Grainger. I often say, "Listen, if you know of a neat ministry or someone I ought to have on the show, let me know." Jim Grainger sent me an email that said, "Dude, you have to have this guy from that heathen pagan station over at KLOS be-cause he's a believer and he's solid. I heard him speak."

We vetted Frank through the team and Frank Sontag got the green light, and now you're here, bro. Welcome aboard. How are you, man?

Me: I can't tell you what an honor it is to be on your show and thank you for your radio ministry. Frank, I'm thrilled to be here.

Frank Pastore: I can't believe we look somewhat alike. You've got no hair like me but a scratchy, fuzzy thing on your chin. Very cool. You're very hip, by the way.

Frank Sontag: Well, you are a little younger and a little better looking than me.

You always want to make the host look good in radio and TV interviews. As for who was better looking, I'll let the reader decide.

◀ That's my dad, Frank Sontag, Jr., standing with his parents, Frank and Stella Sontag, shortly after he made his First Communion. He's dressed all in white. Was he really wearing pantaloons and white stockings?

▲ It's quitting time at Fisher Body, the auto parts factory in Cleveland, circa 1940s. My grandfather and namesake, Frank Sontag, is holding a bottle of brew and looking to the camera while a dice gambling game is played. My grandfather was the son of Italian immigrants who arrived at Ellis Island at the start of the 20th century.

I have one sibling, my sister, ▶
Theresa, who's two years
older than me. We're lucky
to be born because our
mother suffered multiple
miscarriages early in her
marriage.

That's my grandmother, whom I called Nana, sharing a Christmastime moment with a good friend, Sam Paventi. My grandparents were always having friends and family over for long Sunday afternoon meals.

I was in the second grade, still seven years old, when I received my First Communion. I'm standing in the back row to the very right. Father McNally is seated in the front.

I attended St. Joseph's Elementary in Cleveland during my grammar school days, a time when nuns wore heavy black habits and were as mean as can be. There was none more spiteful than Sister Patrick Marie, who's standing in the back of my second grade class. If she wasn't throwing erasers at me for daydreaming out the window, she was calling me to come forward and get paddled for some act of malfeasance.

I was a small kid growing up
and wanted to become a race
horse jockey. I was almost six
years old when this shot was
taken in June 1961.

Dad was a robust figure in my life as we stand in our
Cleveland neighborhood. This shot was taken in April
1963 when I was seven years old.

Get that kid some accordion lessons! My parents bought me a squeezebox when I was eight years old
and paid for lessons. I even placed third in an Ohio state competition. Once the Beatles hit in 1964,
though, all I wanted to play was the guitar.

I was confirmed in the Catholic Church when I was in third grade. Standing with me is my teacher, Miss Lange, whom I had a crush on. I was heartbroken when she got married during our school year. I thought we were going to be husband and wife.

Mom raised me as a Catholic, which included all the trappings of faith: the folded hands, the prayer missal, and the rosary beads wrapped around my wrists. By the time I graduated from an all-boys Catholic high school, however, I had rejected Catholicism and started my own search to find God.

Nerd alert! When I skipped fourth grade, I checked all the boxes for class nerd. I was the bright-looking kid with slick brown hair and black horn-rimmed glasses. The only thing missing was white tape across the bridge of my glasses and a pocket protector.

I found out that you don't want to wear glasses when you play Little League baseball. Infielders yelled "Hey, Four Eyes!" in their chatter whenever I came to the plate.

Dad was well-liked in Hollywood, where he was a lighting director. He got to hang out with stars like Carol Burnett and Walter Matthau, who hammed it up with my father in this classic photo. I think Pops won the hairy chest contest here.

Dad often had to go on out-town shoots. Here he's on location for the 1970 disaster movie, *Airport*, which starred Burt Lancaster, Dean Martin, George Kennedy, and Jean Seberg.

After we moved to California, Dad took me deer hunting. He was a man's man with a woolly six-pack. That's Mom standing with us.

Prom night! I took Sally Moran ▶
to my senior prom at Notre
Dame High, which was an all-
boys school. We weren't dating,
but she agreed to go with me
because she heard a famous
teen actor was going to be there,
and she was an aspiring actress.

A year after high school graduation, ▶
a childhood friend named Chris
asked me to be her escort for her
senior prom. I had a growth spurt
after I graduated from high school
because I was a year younger than
the rest of my class. Notice my
classic mutton-chop sideburns that
were fashionable in the early '70s.

◀ My parents got divorced as I was graduating high school. After their break-up, Mom was a survivor. She went to beauty college and started cutting hair to make ends meet.

◀ During my twenties, I played in a lot of city basketball leagues and even semi-pro ball. Basketball was my love, and check out the short shorts back in the day.

This is where it all happened on the *Impact* show, which I hosted for twenty-one years at KLOS every Sunday night from midnight to 5 a.m. This was a show for those interested in spirituality and self-discovery.

▲

In the 1990s, the *Los Angeles Times* called me a "New Age guru," which was recognition of my public persona. I lectured on spirituality a couple of times of a month and often spoke at the Philosophical Research Society in Los Feliz, an affluent neighborhood in central L.A.

I took an *Easy Rider* road trip with Michael Benner, the host of the *Impact* radio show on KLOS, in 1987. We rode from L.A. to the Grand Canyon on Suzuki 850s, a 1,000-mile round trip. I had the beard and long hair going at the time.

I was a part-time dad for my daughter, Lindsay, who grew up, for the most part, in Las Vegas with her mother. I loved it when Lindsay stayed with me for extended visits.

Surrounded by "carts" in the KLOS studio, where songs and commercials were recorded on for easy play, my producer Al Rische lays a wet one on me.

▼

▲

In addition to hosting the *Impact* show on Sunday nights, I was also the engineer for the *Mark & Brian Show*, heard weekdays on KLOS during morning drive time from 6-10 a.m. Mark and Brian were a rock 'n' rolling crew for twenty-five years. From the left, Mark Thompson, Lee Smelser (longtime basketball coach at College of the Canyons), Preva Lohla (a sidekick on the show) Brian Phelps (with his arm around me), and a great friend, Jeff Dunlap, line up for a shot. I coached Jeff when he played high school ball in 1979, and he went on to become a college basketball coach. Today, he's director of operations for the North Carolina State University basketball team.

Erin and I
have enjoyed
many fun
times together,
including this
trip to Hanalei
Bay on the
"Garden Island"
of Kauai.

Erin and I were married in
Laguna Beach on December 29,
2004, where we honeymooned
for a few days. Our wedding was
small—just two friends who
acted as witnesses—but that's
the way we wanted it.

Our son, Dante, was born on
February 12, 2008, bringing
us great joy as well as the
challenges of raising a son.

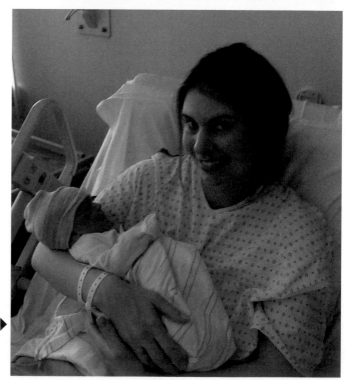

In 2001, I hired Tracy Thackrah as my screener for *Impact*, my call-in talk show. Tracy and I became good friends. He wasn't a Christian at the time, but after going through drug rehab, he became a follower of Christ—and would later have a huge impact on me.

On December 17, 2009, Dale Thackrah and his brother, Tracy, had an agenda: Confront me with the claims of Christ following a golf game at the Fullerton Municipal Golf Course.

After Erin decided to give her life to
Christ in the summer of 2011, she got
baptized at Carpinteria State Beach.

On the last day the Mark & Brian Show aired
on KLOS on August 17, 2012, Erin took
this shot inside the studio during the final
moments. No media were allowed, so Erin
had the only picture, which was published in
various newspapers. Minutes after we signed
off for the final time, the general manager
told me to clean out my locker—I was done.

Oh, happy days . . . Erin and
I were tickled to celebrate
the wedding of my daughter,
Lindsay, in 2013.

◀ Our son, Dante . . . I can't describe how much it means to me that he knows Jesus at such a young age.

▲ A family shot taken at the Salem company picnic at Universal Studios. (KKLA is owned by Salem Communications, which has around 100 radio stations in thirty-four markets.)

◀ This photo of my father, Frank Sontag, and my stepmom, Anita, means a lot to me. This shot was taken during the Thanksgiving holiday in 2013—the last time I saw my dad. He passed away on March 31, 2014.

A dream come true . . . owning a horse. ▶ Actually, Foolin' is a thoroughbred who raced in Southern California and did well during his career. He's now retired and living the good life at my father and stepmom's ranch in Idaho.

My story is eerily similar to that of Frank Pastore, a former Cincinnati Reds pitcher who got into broadcasting and was the host of a popular talk show on KKLA in Los Angeles.

After having us on his radio show, Frank Pastore took this shot of Erin and me on his Honda motorcycle.

What a prince of a guy, Frank Pastore. I loved this dear brother in Christ.

Waiting to go back on the air inside the KKLA broadcast studio . . . and reminding myself how grateful I am for the opportunity the Lord has given me to be on the air.

Frank Pastore: (laughs out loud): Good answer! He sucks up right from the beginning. So you're from Cleveland, the accordion thing. You still into music?

Me: I wanted a guitar growing up. I grew up with the Beatles, and my parents stuck me with an accordion. I had a permanent black and blue bruise on my chest from eight to nine years of age. I hated the accordion. Finally, I said no more. I don't play music anymore, even though I love listening to music.

Yeah, we came out here from Cleveland in '65, as you said. I remember the first thing I wanted to do was go to the beach. I had never seen a beach before. Lake Erie was our body of water, and as you all know the joke, Lake Erie caught on fire because it was so polluted and disgusting back then.

So we went to the beach, and I felt, *Wow, California. I'm here.* Went to Notre Dame High School. All-boy Catholic school. Raised in Catholicism.

Frank Pastore: Me, too.

Me: I remember that summer, when I graduated in 1972, my thought was I was never going to go to church again. I just didn't feel it. I didn't like church. So from that time on, through my twenties, I wandered. I was lost. Did a lot of different things. Lot of different jobs. You know what it was like in your twenties—which happened yesterday. Life was so right there, and you felt like you had life by the tail.

You mentioned my crash. That's where I want to start this. It was June 17, 1984. I'm in the San Fernando Valley on my motorcycle. No helmet laws back then, so I wasn't wearing a helmet. I did have hair—long hair—to fly in the breeze.

Frank Pastore: What kind of bike?

> **Frank Sontag:** It was a little dinky Honda FT 350. Single stroke. I'm driving on the 101, coming up Balboa, and there's a long straightaway there . . .

And that's how I started my description of how a Corvette roared up my tailpipe and mowed me down. I didn't mention having a passenger on the back of the bike—Heather. It was a complicating detail that would involve another five minutes of explanation, and our time was limited. You're always on the clock in radio.

After I finished describing the collision, Frank said this:

> **Frank Pastore:** You were on a little 350 without a helmet. Dude, are you kidding? You're lucky to be alive!

> **Me:** Well, yeah, that was my proverbial wake-up call.

I then I recounted how I sold everything I owned and move to Lake Tahoe to sort things out. What happened to me on the 101? How did I survive the horrible accident?

> **Me:** Frank, I had no broken bones. I had nothing but road rash. But I had no relationship with God whatever. I had walked away from the church some twelve years earlier.

> **Frank Pastore:** Did you believe in God?

> **Me:** Remember, I was raised a Catholic, so I believed in God, whatever that meant.

> **Frank Pastore:** That would have gotten you a B on the Christianity 101 multiple-choice exam.

> **Me:** Probably a C-minus.

> **Frank Pastore:** So you believed in God but had no personal relationship. You weren't into organized religion. Would you consider yourself, at that point, a spiritual person?

Frank Sontag: I *began* to perceive myself as a spiritual person. Like I said, I locked myself inside a cabin in Sunnyside in Lake Tahoe, in the middle of winter, and I started to read books. It was weird, Frank. I graduated from high school when I was sixteen, and I learned to dumb down because I had skipped the fourth grade. I became a jock. Learned to play basketball and got stupid. So after this crash, I decided to start reading everything I could get my hands on. I found Gandhi and Dr. Martin Luther King. New Age authors. After a handful of months up there, freezing with no heat, I decided to come back to L.A.

Here's where I told Frank that I happened to turn on the radio one night and heard Michael Benner say, "Motorcycle crashes are transformational." And then I described how I hooked up with Michael and eventually took over his job as host of *Impact*, which was a miracle in itself.

Frank Pastore: No way!

Me: As a guy who dropped out of college, who was terrified to take a speech class, I was behind a microphone, like we are right now, hosting a late night show on KLOS that was on the air for twenty-one years.

Frank Pastore: Dude, stop—we have to take a break. When we come back, we're going to continue with Frank Sontag. If you're a fan of KLOS, then you know a bit about him. Frank Sontag is sharing his story today. You're the on-air technical engineer for *Mark & Brian*—is that right?

Me: Yeah.

Frank Pastore: When we come back, we'll continue with Frank's story with how he came to Christ in December 2009, when his life got really interesting. We'll find out why when we come back.

That was a nice teaser. Frank was a real pro. Then his engineer had some fun at my expense. When we came out of the break, the bumper music was an accordion version of the Disney tune, "It's a Small World," which was an amusing touch. During the next segment, I related my testimony from December 17, 2009 when I was playing golf with the Thackrah brothers. When I finished, Frank said this:

> **Frank Pastore:** I love genuine testimonies. They aren't churched up. Frank Sontag . . . I'm just hearing this story for the first time like you guys are. What's neat about this is that it's not like you're a "professional Christian" yet. It's only been less than two-and-a-half years.
>
> So I'm trying to do the math in my head. What age were you when you became a Christian? Fifty-five?
>
> **Me:** Let's see. In 2009, I was fifty-four.
>
> **Frank Pastore:** That's my age now. So for fifty-four years, you lived without Him, and now His grace has overwhelmed you. So let's open up the phone lines. It's Jenna in Anaheim. What would you like to say to Frank Sontag, who did the *Impact* show for twenty-one years?
>
> **Jenna in Anaheim:** I just wanted to tell you that I listen to KLOS in the morning and KKLA in the afternoon. What a dichotomy that is. I was listening the morning Dante was born. I remember that like it was yesterday. I was so touched by that. Also, I wanted to encourage you to be a good witness to Mark and Brian.
>
> **Me:** My son was a radio star a minute and a half after he was born.
>
> **Frank Pastore:** Really?
>
> **Me:** We were in the birthing room. My wife was shaking her head, saying, "What are you doing?" But I called Mark and Brian anyway, and we were put on the air. I

introduced Dante to the world. He was crying his way on the air.

Frank Pastore: I love it! That's awesome. Let's go to Cassandra in Tujunga. Good afternoon, Cassandra. What do you want to say to Frank Sontag?

Cassandra in Tujunga: I remember listening to you in 1994 on the *Impact* show, when I was sixteen years old. I grew up with the Lord, but fell away. I always wondered if you were a Christian. Praise God for your walk. I used to do dope at that time. I'm free of drugs now. I've been walking with the Lord for four years. I'm a baby Christian myself.

I just want to say the way you and Frank Pastore conduct yourselves on the air, you are very similar. You have so much integrity. This is so awesome, so God bless you.

Me: I'm pretty stoked and excited about where I go from here. I'm all in with Him.

Frank Pastore: Let's go to Betty in Ventura. Betty, say hi to Frank Sontag.

Betty in Ventura: I have a question . . . now that you're a Christian, is it difficult for you to work on the *Mark & Brian Show*? They are a little off-color. I find now that I'm a Christian, sometimes I can't really listen.

Frank Sontag: The answer to your question is yes. They're great guys. They're really nice guys. I love them. But yes, it is difficult. That's all I can say. It is a bit of a challenge.

We ran out of time. The hour had passed by so quickly.

I loved Frank and how he hosted his show with enthusiasm. It felt good to be in his hands. Coming out of one of the breaks, he recapped how similar our stories were. When he threw a pitch to Steve Sax at Dodger Stadium, the date was June 6, 1984. "And eleven days later, Frank Sontag is riding a motorcycle on the 101 at Balboa," he said, his voice trailing off.

We were both blown away that God had used traumatic, life-changing events in *the same month* nearly three decades earlier to set us down a path toward accepting Him as our Lord and Savior.

As he wrapped up the fast-paced hour for the KKLA audience, Frank promised to bring me back on the air soon.

He proved to be a man of his word.

20

DON'T STOP BELIEVING

A few weeks after I shared my testimony on the *Frank Pastore Show*, Frank's people got in touch with me about the next time I could come back. We agreed on Friday, June 29, during the second hour at 5 p.m.

We picked a doozy of a day. After the *Mark & Brian Show* signed off that morning, Mark Thompson called the staff together and said he had something to say to us. Mark *never* did that, so I knew something was up.

Mark dropped a bombshell: he was leaving the *Mark & Brian Show*, effective August 17. He and his wife, Linda, had purchased a home in scenic Lake Norman, North Carolina, and wanted a change of scenery—as well as an opportunity to get out of the L.A. rat race. They were empty nesters in their mid-fifties, having raised a son and two daughters.

There was another issue on the table—their mortality. Mark was the same age as me, and he told us that guys his age were dropping dead and there were other things he wanted to do before he checked out. He couldn't pursue other opportunities if he was sitting in that morning chair. As for Linda, she had looked death square in the eye five years earlier when she learned she had breast cancer. Aggressive treatments saved her life. Now that her cancer was in remission, it was time to take advantage of the extra years.

The news of Mark Thompson's departure was the first thing that

Frank asked me about later that afternoon on KKLA:

> **Frank Pastore:** A few weeks ago, I had the great Frank Sontag on the show. I didn't know who he was or how important he was. Frank gave his life to Christ on December 17, 2009, so it was just a few years ago. He's with his wife, Erin, in the studio.
>
> Now the big news today is that the *Mark & Brian Show* may be ending because Mark Thompson wants to move back to North Carolina. So dude, get to the good stuff. What's happening with the show?
>
> **Me:** Listen, you're as surprised as I am. We've been hearing rumors, and honestly, I didn't know anything this morning until Mark addressed the staff and said that as of August 17, that was going to be it. I don't know what that means for the future of the show. I've been a small part of it for fifteen years or so, so we'll see. Lord willing, I'll still be employed at KLOS.

And then a thought came to my mind—one that had been turning around in my head. I felt comfortable with Frank, so I thought I'd throw it out there.

> **Me:** I know I would love to do a Christian talk program. Maybe I'll end up here. I don't know.
>
> **Frank Pastore** (grinning): Now that's immediately threatening to me. Dude, we're done. Next!

We shared a long laugh. It was all in good fun. Frank wasn't trying to bust my chops—just the opposite. This was peer-to-peer teasing.

> **Frank Pastore:** I'd love to have you as part of the family here on KKLA. But for people who are big fans of the *Mark & Brian Show,* they're wondering what's happening.
>
> **Me:** Mark and Brian are great guys. I'm very close with

both. I love them both immensely. Linda's bout with cancer was a wake-up call. They probably talked about their situation and realized that life is really short.

Part of me wasn't surprised to hear the announcement this morning. It's going to be on Brian's shoulders now. Hopefully, we'll continue. I'm in full trust of the whole process.

I know my dear wife, who is sitting next to me, used to listen to Mark and Brian growing up. This has a huge ripple effect and is a shock to people who are just finding about it.

Frank Pastore: Is there going to be a *Frank & Brian Show*?

That was a pertinent question, given the moment. But as a Christian, I was no longer suited to a morning show that relied on sexual banter between the hosts. On top of that, I didn't have the skill set to write risqué material.

Me: There won't be a *Frank & Brian Show*, as far as I know. Brian will continue to be the captain. Hopefully I can play a small part and still have my foot in radio.

My passion is talk radio—doing what you do. I did *Impact* for twenty-one years on Sunday nights. I miss doing the show. I haven't done it for about three years. These days, doing a morning drive program in major-market radio is about the yucks and the funnies.

Frank Pastore: And they have an incredibly loyal audience. I've never listened to the show, so I don't want to pretend that I have. Time to switch gears. So you've been a Christian for two-and-a-half years. How's it going?

Me: Well, it depends on what day you talk to me. Most times it's good, but just when you think you have it down, the Enemy strikes. It's been a struggle, as I said on your program last time.

I was about to continue when Frank interrupted that it was time for a traffic and commercial break. While we were off the air, I brought Frank up to speed on where Erin and I were—in the deep weeds. Coming out of the break, Frank said this:

> **Frank Pastore:** I wish you could have heard what we talked about the last two minutes or so. Frank and Erin are so transparent and so real in their relationship and their walk with Christ. You rarely hear this these days. I don't want to talk out of school here, but typically on KKLA, it's sermon shows all day long—and then me. Those of you who are struggling and don't want the academic, apologetic answer, you're asking, *How do I deal with what I'm going through?*

Then Frank turned to Erin, who was sitting next to me, behind her own microphone in the studio.

> **Frank Pastore:** Where were you spiritually, Erin, before Frank became a Christian? Be brutally honest.

> **Erin:** Part of his appeal to me back then was that he was a broad, spiritual man, very accepting of all faiths. I was with him and felt the same way. When he gave his life to Christ, though, I thought he was nuts. I thought he was going through a mid-life crisis. I didn't know what to do with it. I was angry because I felt that he didn't take my needs into account. I felt he was moving away from me. That set off a hard time for us, almost to the point where we divorced. Things were bad.

> **Frank Pastore:** Did he have to sleep on the couch? I'm prying, but I want people to understand what really happened.

> **Erin:** It was really bad. I probably hit my bottom. At that point, he had found Reality Church in Carpinteria. He said, "Erin, come with me." I was so desperate for anything that I went with him. I fell in love with his church.

Frank Pastore: Wait. You're into the all the Eastern stuff—mysticism, Taoism, etc. But dudette, he's going to Reality Church in Carpinteria. He asks you to go. So why did you go?

Erin: At that point, we were into counseling because we had decided that we wanted to make our marriage work. Counseling helped. But there was this desperation for something bigger than myself. The other things in my life were not working.

When I went to Reality Church, I started to be fed. Then Frank bought me a Bible, and I couldn't put it down. Since I was raised Catholic, part of me felt that I was coming home when I read the Bible. When Religious Science was my thing, I never felt like it was enough.

Frank Pastore: In Religious Science, God is not a Supreme Being but a Force. Would you pray?

Erin: Sure, all the time.

Frank Pastore: Who was listening?

Erin: The one God, the Creator of everything.

Frank Pastore: In the Eastern religions, God is not a personal being. It's a Force. There is no God. There is no heaven. There's no life after death. You just pop out of existence and nothing becomes nothing.

The reason why I asked you the prayer thing and the reason it caught you is because you were praying largely because of your Catholic roots. The thing with Religious Science and "mind" cults is that you have to get back in sync with the "energy field" and "energy force." Hence all the New Age and Harmonic Convergence and the crystals and pyramid stuff.

But you never felt fulfilled by that.

Erin: That's right. I was told that if you think positively, positive things will happen. But how often can you do that? It doesn't happen like that.

Frank Pastore: Please don't exaggerate this. Did you ever have that sense of fulfillment or warmth or glow at any time when you were into the Religious Science stuff?

Erin: You know, I felt connected on some level, but it never lasted beyond those brief moments. Since I've become a Christian, I don't feel that "aaah" moment all the time. It's not an easy walk at all times. But I keep going because I see the miracles happening.

Frank Pastore: That's great to hear. Name one.

Erin: Our marriage for one. We have had a lot of obstacles. We have a big age difference. With that comes a hard dynamic. But our marriage is better now.

Frank Pastore: Did Frank become a better man and husband?

Erin: Oh, yes. Before he gave his life to Christ, he was very stubborn and full of his own opinions. That was one of the things that caused us to drift apart. After he gave his life to Christ, he became much more open and even exuberant, like many do. He wouldn't stop talking about what Christ was doing in his life, and that caused a rift between us. After we went through everything, he had to back off to keep me interested. When I was able to find Christ on my own, that's when everything started to change. But yes, he has become a much more humble man. He's much more loving.

I watched and listened, humbled and on the verge of tears. I was fascinated by Erin's conversation with Frank and the transparency springing forth from my wife. I was so proud of her. Frank then turned the conversation back toward me.

Frank Pastore: So, Frank, there's not going to be a *Frank & Brian Show*. Dude, what are you going to be doing?

Me: Only the Lord knows. I have no clue. I have no idea. My sense is they like me at the station and they'll keep me there. But ever since my walk started a few years ago, I'm like, "Lord, use me for Your glory. Whatever it is and in everything I do."

I really feel called to be a pastor. I don't have a penny saved to my name. The Enemy is very active: *What are you doing? You're an awful provider.*

Spiritual warfare goes on in our house a lot. I don't know what's going to happen, but I pray that I get out of my own way, whatever the plan is.

Frank Pastore: Let me jump in here since you guys are being so vulncrable. Let me ask some probing questions here. When you said, "I don't have a penny to my name," I know you don't own a yacht down at Malibu or have a ton of money. So here's my encouragement to you: Don't go into the pastorate to make money.

Me: I know that.

Frank Pastore: Look, there are some people who say, "I've failed at everything else. God must be calling me into the ministry." Dude, it's not that way at all. Being a pastor is more than delivering three messages on Sunday. Unless you have a counselor's heart, then my encouragement is no, go in a different route.

Look, it doesn't mean you have to be the "pastor" of a church. There are all sorts of pastoral roles that you can fulfill. Dude, just sharing your story like we're doing now, is something you could do. Erin, you're nodding your head. He's good at this, right?

Erin: He's in his element. I cried when I listened to his interview with you on KKLA six weeks ago. It was a beautiful thing. He's just great behind a microphone. I could see him doing some sort of pastoral thing on the radio.

When we were done at the top of the six o'clock hour, Erin and I said our thank yous and our goodbyes. Frank was having none of it.

"Don't leave, don't leave," he said. So we stayed and hung out while Frank interviewed, by phone, Dr. Frank Turek, an author and Christian apologist who'd debated atheist Christopher Hitchens twice on university campuses. A lot of Franks that day for Frank.

When Frank was finished, he walked us to the parking garage next to the California Credit Union Building. We came upon his mode of transportation—a Honda VTX 1800. I whistled in appreciation. This was a big bike with a muscular body long and low to the ground. My old Honda FT500 looked like a toy scooter compared to Frank's chrome-heavy motorcycle with a purple gas tank and fiberglass trim.

Frank was proud of his Honda VTX 1800 and talked of his love for motorcycle trips. He said he liked riding to Scottsdale, Arizona, which prompted me to tell him about my trip to the Grand Canyon years earlier aboard Michael Benner's Suzuki 850.

"Yeah, there's nothing like it, riding the open road," Frank said. "Gina gives me grief, though, about riding the freeways here," he said. "When I bought my bike, she got pretty upset, but I told her, 'Look, life is life, and you're gonna go when you're gonna go.' I'm not a reckless rider. I ride very safe."

I asked him if he lane-split on the freeways.

"Are you kidding? With this bike?"

"I guess not. I never did it when I used to ride."

Frank had an idea. "Why don't you and Erin get on the bike? I'll take a picture of you. For old times."

Erin looked at me and smiled. She was glad that this was as close as I was getting to a motorcycle. I handed Frank my iPhone, and we sat on his Honda and posed.

I still have that photo today.

A RETURN VISIT

Ever since I came on the *Frank Pastore Show* in April, I felt compelled to share my story with people who *never* listen to Christian radio—those who attend lectures at the Philosophical Research Society, searching for God.

At first, I ran into some headwinds when I called the PRS director, who knew me but hadn't heard from me in a couple of years. Maybe he *did* listen to KKLA because he asked me pointblank what I wanted to talk about. I said I had become a Christian, but I didn't want to preach from the Bible or anything. I just wanted to talk about what happened to me and where my life was now.

I heard a long pause. I knew that a buzzword at the Philosophical Research Society was being "tolerant" of other beliefs. Would tolerance be shown toward Christianity?

The answer, surprisingly, was yes. When I spoke at the Philosophical Research Society on Monday night, July 2, I was pleased to see eighty or ninety souls had shown up for my lecture. Maybe they were expecting the old *Impact* host to riff on human potential again.

The last thing I wanted to do was hit people over the head with Christ. Instead, I simply shared my story, much like the Apostle Paul did when given an audience in the Book of Acts. I did not preach the usual, *We are all powerful. We can create anything in life. It's just a matter of emphasizing the emotion.*

Instead, I spoke sincerely and forthrightly: "This is what happened to me. This is where my life is now. Christ is my Savior. He is in control."

Some people were in tears. Some were not happy. And the rest probably left wondering what the heck they just heard. But I was really glad to get my story out there to a New Age audience. My prayer was to plant seeds.

During a Q&A, a KLOS fan asked me what would happen to the *Mark & Brian Show* when Mark Thompson left on August 17.

I repeated the same answer I gave Frank Pastore earlier: I had no idea.

It was all in the Lord's hands.

21

THESE BOOTS ARE
MADE FOR WALKIN'

After twenty-five years on the air, the final week of the *Mark & Brian Show* felt like a countdown. I knew Brian Phelps was in negotiations with Cumulus Media to remain with KLOS and bring in a new co-host.

Something had to break. *Mark & Brian* was the longest-running morning radio program in Los Angeles, so a new variant of the show would have a built-in audience. The rumors of who would replace Mark were as common as the mice that ran unfettered up and down the hallways of the KLOS studios. One of the names tossed around was Jill Whelan, a childhood actress who played the role of Vicki Stubing, the daughter of Captain Merrill Stubing on the TV series, *The Love Boat*. Since then, Jill had been doing some improv comedy and working on-air at a Philadelphia AM station. The break room gossip was that they'd make a deal and launch the *Brian & Jill Show*.

The night before the final broadcast on Friday, August 17, I was getting ready for bed at my customary 8:30 p.m., looking forward to seven hours of sleep. It was going to be a big day. I was nervous about what lay ahead.

My iPhone buzzed. Brian Phelps was calling. My heart leaped because I knew this could be the big news I was waiting for. A last-second agreement had been struck.

"I'm out," Brian said. "We couldn't get it done."

I was stunned. The show was over. *Poof.*

Now that Brian was out of the picture, everything was up in the air. I hung onto previous assurances from management that the entire staff would be re-signed, no matter the outcome of negotiations. Since KLOS couldn't come to terms with Brian, I figured they'd reshuffle the deck and bring in a new comedy team. Starting over with new morning drive hosts would be fine with me. I liked my job. Needed the paycheck.

The final installment of the *Mark & Brian Show* was as emotional as you'd think it would be. There was none of the usual looseness or jocularity. Plenty of gallows humor, though. Throughout the somber morning, Mark and Brian took emotional calls from local dignitaries and famous celebrities. As the minutes clicked off during the final hour, Mark and Brian invited staffers like myself to say our last words.

I had given a great deal of thought about what I would say, if given the microphone. I knew full well there was a huge difference between the KKLA audience and those who listened to a secular station like KLOS. Mark and Brian knew I was a Christian because I had told them about my life-changing experience on December 17, 2009. Hopefully, they saw me as a different person, but that didn't stop Mark from getting in little digs every now and then:

Frank doesn't gamble anymore because he's a Christian.

We can't party with Frank anymore, not after he became a holy roller.

Watch your language, everyone. You don't want to say anything to hurt Frank's ears.

This holy roller rolled with it. I was taking the high road. If given the chance to speak on the air during the final show, I wanted to be a witness for Christ. When Brian threw it to me, here's what I said, the nerves tumbling forth with each sentence:

> **Me:** It's only by God's good grace that I've had the fortune . . . [I started to break down here] . . . and blessings to sit with two of the most incredible men . . . [I stopped to catch my breath] . . . for the last fifteen-plus years. It's been the highlight of my life professionally. I don't know what the future holds, but I do know who holds my future.
>
> I want to thank Danny and Ted and Preva and Billy

and Kelly for putting up with me. And I just want to tell you two guys that I wish you well. I'll be praying for you and hope to keep in touch with you. I'm so grateful for my wife and my son. I'm grateful for Jesus Christ, who is my Lord and Savior. I couldn't go through what I've gone through the last few years without Him.

I love you guys more than words can express. L.A. is so blessed and so lucky to have witnessed the talents and the joys you've put into so many people's hearts that you will never even know. So from the bottom of my heart, I thank you so much for being my friend and for enriching my career by letting me sit here and participate. Listening to you every day has put a smile on my face. Thank you.

Brian Phelps: Frankie, no one has experienced what I have experienced over the last three months, except for you. The frustration I spoke of earlier about negotiations . . . we have always been very close from the beginning. Because of these tough times and you seeing what I have been going through, you have become a best friend and you always will be to me. I love you very, very much, man.

After the final, final sign-off—the last *Mark & Brian Show* ran forty minutes long—there was a long exhale from everyone. We were done. The twenty-five-year-long run was history.

The general manager poked his head into the studio. "Everyone to my office. Five minutes."

A half dozen staffers and I marched into the GM's office. My heart was in my throat. He spoke unemotionally and without preamble. "Pack your stuff. You have a half-hour to clean out your lockers."

And don't let the door hit you on the way out.

This was the latest example of corporate radio—soulless corporations cleaning house and starting over with new personnel . . . at lower salaries. The severance package was short, the equivalent of three-and-a-half months of pay.

Four days later, Cumulus Media—who'd purchased Citadel—

announced that the *Heidi & Frank Show* would replace Mark and Brian, starting Monday, September 4. That was quick. And I was not the "Frank."

The new hosts were Heidi Hamilton and Frank Kramer, who'd done shows together on Star 98.7 FM and KLSX 97.1 FM. They were cut from the same racy cloth as morning shows on all metro rock stations. Frank liked to rattle on about his pot-smoking and Heidi was animated when chatting up her lesbian encounters.

Maybe it was good I got fired.

BACK IN THE STUDIO

Five weeks after being fired, Frank Pastore brought Erin and me back into the studio. This is what transpired on September 28, 2012, inside the KKLA studios:

> **Frank Pastore:** Happy Friday, everybody. Welcome back to the *Frank Pastore Show*. Joining us in the studio are Frank and Erin Sontag. For those of you who are fans of KLOS, you may remember years ago when Frank Sontag had his own talk show. He's been involved in Southern California radio for almost thirty years now. He had been the board-op engineer for the *Mark & Brian Show*, and they've recently gone off the air.
>
> The neat thing—not about going off the air—for Frank and Erin is that they both have become Christians. I want everyone to know this: Truly, I have no clue what's happened to them since the show ended. But I want to know Erin, before we ask Frank, how you're doing?
>
> **Erin:** We're doing okay. It's been a month now since he lost his job at KLOS. It came as a shock. He was there for twenty-seven years. We thought he was going to be re-signed, possibly for a raise, but five minutes after the *Mark & Brian Show* was over, he was let go.
>
> We've had a lot of God moments since then. We know that we're on the right path. But we've had tough moments that have really challenged our faith. We're working through it.

Frank Pastore: The last I heard was that there was going to be another show. Then there was this gigantic gear-change kind of thing. . .

Erin: We found out the night before the final show, 8:30 at night. Got a phone call, so we braced ourselves.

Frank Pastore: Wow. So, buddy, what happened, man?

Me: I go in on Friday morning, under the auspices of saying goodbye on the air, thinking we would be reassigned. Five minutes after the show ended, we were called into the GM's office. He said, "Thank you. The show is done. Clean your lockers."

It's not like I expected some big thank you for twenty-seven years because I've seen too many good people let go in corporate radio in a blink of an eye. I wasn't happy with the way everything was handled, but what can you do?

The first couple of weeks were a little rough. Erin is being gracious on the air, but we've had a tough go the last month. I don't want to be too politically incorrect here, but women like to know that they are being taken care of. Now this is the first time I've been out of a gig.

It's been five weeks, and I've interviewed at different radio stations. I talked to your good boss here, Chuck Tyler, a really nice guy. Nothing out there. I'm still not cashing a check, so we're leaning hard on the Lord. I know it's easy to say that the Lord will never forsake you and the Lord takes care of everything, but then the reality of life in the flesh hits sometimes. Life gets to be a bit daunting.

Frank Pastore: Dude, you need to know I completely sympathize with this because as a former baseball player, I never had a skill where I could get a job anywhere. I was a baseball player, and that's really niche. You can't get people out, you're unemployed. That was me.

Then for me it was going to seminary and doing the apologetics thing, but if a church doesn't ask you to come speak, you don't have a paying gig. And now I'm doing radio. It's not like I'm a dentist or an architect or an engineer. So I get it that it's a real sort of a niche thing, and we need to be grateful for the jobs we do have. But as of right now, you're still looking.

Me: Yeah. My first choice is to stay in radio. I've been doing it for most of my adult life. As I said on my sign-off, I didn't know what the future holds but I knew who held my future.

Just thinking about it, I get a little choked up. Look, bottom line, we have no control in life. Adversity happens. Only the Lord knows what's going to happen from here.

Frank Pastore: One of the things I want to encourage you on is this: Continue to ask the questions. And to pursue. And to be honest. Don't fake it at all. Be raw, as you have been. I mean, you're still unemployed.

Erin, I remember when I got released from the Cincinnati Reds. I tried to suck it up and act like it didn't hurt, but watching my wife saying, "What are we going to do now?" and crying night after night hurt a lot. We had some money put away in the bank. And then we got a letter from the IRS saying we had to come up with all this money. It rocked our world. And we were Christians.

Erin: Interesting. When Frank was let go, we had this moment of clarity. *Okay, we know it's time to move on and do God's work.* We had a lot of calm, and then the reality hit. Now we're fighting panic mode a lot of the time. We have Dante. He's in school. We have a house payment. I know that things will work out, but the uncertainty is really hard to deal with.

We're going through it and doing the best that we can. We're showing up every day. We're more involved with our church, which has been great.

Frank Pastore: Frank, are you willing to move?

Me: That's been asked of me. I don't know. I've been in L.A. for so long. I've met a lot of people. I don't know, but I will not immediately say, "Absolutely not. I will not move."

Frank Pastore: Good. Let me extend an invitation to the audience. What advice would you share to Frank and Erin Sontag? Remember, they are new Christians, and they don't want silly and plastic and fake and phony. Nor do I.

What advice out of your life experience would you share with them? Let's go to Leland in Glendora.

Leland in Glendora: Once you get comfortable with being uncomfortable, like in the situation you're in right now, that's when God moves. He certainly did that in my life.

Me: I don't know what Proverb it is, but it keeps going through my head—Trust in the Lord with all your heart and lean not on your own understanding.

Frank Pastore: There's no shortcuts. Sorry, that's the way it is. Sheri in Wilmington, what do you want to say to the Sontags?

Sheri: I want to encourage you. I lost my job due to my disability and lost my income. Then my husband lost his job. This started in 2006. I thought it was a blessing in disguise because it allowed me to pursue my passion.

But things weren't working out for me. I learned to trust God. I still tithed. If someone gave me $20, I tithed from that.

Erin: Frank is a changed man because of Christ. I looked at him the day he was let go from work. He handled it with so much grace and courage. And if this was two years ago, he would have been freaking out. He would have been angry, bitter. He didn't do that.

I appreciated hearing from the listeners. Our final segment was coming to an end. Frank finished by telling this story:

> **Frank Pastore:** Maybe you've heard the "Footprints in the Sand" story. It goes basically like this. When difficult times come in your life, the story is told of a man walking on the beach. He noticed that there were two sets of footprints because God was walking along besides him.
>
> Then he went through a difficult period in his life, and he looked back and saw only one set of footprints in the sand. He was mad. He was angry. He said, "God, you left me. You abandoned me."
>
> Here's the voice that he heard. "No, son, I love you. It was then that I was carrying you."
>
> That speaks to what my callers are saying. So, look, we are going to follow you guys and see what the Lord will do in your lives.

DROPPING IN

A few weeks after Frank Pastore had us on, I felt prompted to call Chuck Tyler to follow up. Maybe something had opened up at KKLA. Chuck was really nice. "Come on down," he said.

In the middle of October, I was sitting in Chuck's office when Frank Pastore passed through the hallways. When he saw me shooting the breeze with Chuck, he stopped in his tracks and poked his nose inside the door.

"What are you doing here?" he asked with a sly grin.

Before I could answer, he pointed at me and said, "You're not taking my job, are you?" Then he laughed.

Chuck and I chuckled as well. This was a case of Frank being his usual playful self. I wasn't sitting with Chuck angling to get Frank's job. I was talking to him about *any* radio job at KKLA, either behind the mic or working the engineer's board.

This was the second time that Frank spoke cryptically about me. The first occasion happened a few months earlier when Frank came home after having Erin and me on the June 29 show.

Frank rode his Honda bike home to Upland and strode into the kitchen, where he hugged his wife, Gina. She was busy preparing dinner.

"Hey, did you hear the Frank Sontag interview today?" he asked.

"Yeah, I listened to a lot of it. Did Erin want to go on the air?"

"Well, not really, but I kinda talked her into it."

Then Frank stopped himself. He looked at Gina and said, "This guy is going to take my job some day."

Gina was startled. Her husband was fifty-five years old and still had many miles left on the odometer. He'd been the host of the *Frank Pastore Show* since January 5, 2004, so he was in the midst of a great run. In every sense, Frank was in the prime of his radio career.

"Are you retiring?" she asked.

"No. Frank's older than me," he said.

"Well then, what do you mean?"

He didn't answer. Gina stood at the kitchen sink and looked at her husband. A little smile came to his face. He said nothing and walked into the hall.

But Frank Pastore must have sensed something.

22

SPIRIT IN THE SKY

November 19, 2012 was a Monday, the start of another work week. But not for me. I still hadn't found a full-time gig in radio. I had my feelers out there, but nothing was happening. Let's face it: when you're fifty-seven years old, no one is banging down your door and demanding you go to work for them. Truth be told, the job outlook was looking bleak.

It was just another work day for Frank Pastore on his KKLA show, billed as the "Intersection of Faith and Reason." During his second hour, shortly after 5 p.m., Frank was getting his teeth into the topic of life after death and what happens to the soul with Dr. Keith Matthews, professor of Spiritual Formation & Contemporary Culture at Azusa Pacific University, twenty miles east of the KKLA studios.

"Is there life after death? Are you more than just your brain?" he asked rhetorically at the start of a monologue. "Are angels real? If everything has a cause, who caused God?"

All good questions and ones he explored with Dr. Matthews. Frank was still animated when he turned the discussion toward a new show on the Science Channel called *Through the Wormhole*, hosted by actor Morgan Freeman. Frank, in a stream of consciousness, riffed some more:

> **Frank Pastore:** Look, you guys know I ride a motorcycle, right? So, at any moment, especially with the idiot people who cross the diamond lane into my lane, all right, without any blinkers—not that I'm angry about it—at any minute I could be spread all over the 210. But that's [just] my body part, and that key distinction undergirds the entire Christian worldview.

A couple of hours later, Frank's show was a wrap at seven o'clock. He gathered his leather shoulder bag and walked to the parking garage, where his Honda VTX 1800 was waiting for him, parked always in the same spot—next to a concrete wall. He strapped on a black Shoei helmet that he had purchased two weeks earlier. Then he pulled onto Central Avenue in Glendale and drove one block to the eastbound on-ramp of the 134 freeway. With Thanksgiving three days away, freeway traffic was light to moderate on this evening—not stop-and-go.

The 134 runs into Interstate 210, a major eight-lane thoroughfare that connects the Pasadena area with suburbs to the east—Arcadia, Monrovia, Azusa, Claremont, and Frank's home in Upland. The 210 has a "diamond lane," a high-occupancy lane dedicated to cars with two or more passengers. Motorcycles are allowed to ride in the diamond lane as well, making the commute much faster during the rush hour.

Frank was cruising along in the diamond lane in Duarte, a few miles before Azusa. He was coming up on Buena Vista Street (Exit 35A) at 7:33 p.m. when a fifty-six-year-old female motorist behind the wheel of a gray Hyundai Sonata lost control of her vehicle and swerved into the diamond lane, striking Frank with such force that he was ejected from his mount.

Frank wasn't as fortunate as I was on the 101 twenty-eight years earlier. His body struck the median concrete barrier with full force, knocking off the visor and a gold cross around his neck. Even though the black Shoei stayed on, he suffered major head injuries. (The gold cross was never found.)

Paramedics quickly arrived on the scene, but Frank's injuries were so extensive that the decision was made to call in a helicopter and transport him to the Los Angeles County USC Medical Center. The driver of the Hyundai Sonata, who was from nearby Glendora, was not injured. (She also turned out to be a nurse and a Frank Pastore fan, and she was not cited.) The collision shut down all eastbound lanes for about an hour, so this was a big deal.

I knew nothing about this terrible tragedy on the evening of November 19. The following morning, Erin and I were about to step inside a church office for a counseling session. I stopped her.

"Wait a second. It's really weird, but I have this sense that I'm supposed to call KKLA."

"Call," she said without hesitation. We both knew that the Holy Spirit often prompted us to do certain things.

I was scanning for my contacts, looking for Chuck Tyler's name, when I received an incoming call. It was Chuck Tyler, the KKLA program director.

The timing of his phone call freaked me out, so I let Chuck go to voice mail. Then I immediately played his message: "Frank, give me a buzz as soon a possible. I have an important question to ask you."

When I called back, he told me that Frank went down in a motorcycle accident the night before. I was blown away—and immediately concerned about Frank and his family.

"Would you be willing to fill in for Frank?" he asked.

"Of course. I'll do anything."

Chuck asked if I could work on Thanksgiving Day from 4-7 p.m. Again, there was no hesitation on my part. Erin and I would figure out something else for Thanksgiving dinner.

After I hung up, I did a news search on my iPhone and read about the traffic accident on the 210. Frank was listed in critical condition after suffering major head injuries. The story also noted that he was in a coma. I felt nauseous after hearing the news.

On Thanksgiving Day, it was quiet inside the KKLA offices in Glendale; a skeleton crew was working. I'll admit that it did feel surreal to sit on Frank's side of the broadcast table and speak into *his* microphone, but at the same time, I knew this was a time to be professional. There were tens of thousands of listeners waiting out there, many motoring on L.A.'s 572 miles of freeways. Thanksgiving is actually a busy travel day as families are either driving to or from loved ones. Here's how I started the show on Thanksgiving Day:

> **Me:** 99.5 KKLA Los Angeles and on the web at kkla.com, we are here on the *Frank Pastore Show*, the intersection of faith and reason every Monday through Friday from 4-7.

Happy Thanksgiving to one and all. My name is Frank Sontag, and I'm sitting in for Frank, whom many of you are holding closely in prayer right now. If you don't know by now, Monday evening, after his program, Frank was involved in a motorcycle accident. He is in serious condition, and we are holding him close in prayer.

I'll admit that I nearly lost it here. I had this fleeting thought of Frank in a hospital room, in a coma, hanging on for life, surrounded by grieving family members. What a horrible Thanksgiving it had to be for them.

Me: Now, some of you may know me. Some of you may not know me. I'm going to assume for the next three hours that a lot of you don't know me. I'm going to attempt to share a little bit about my life.

First of all, at the prominent part of the beginning here, I'm going to talk about my relationship with Frank and the way it happened. A number of months ago, actually, it was December '09, so we're talking nearly thirty-six months ago, I gave my life to Christ. Maybe as the show goes on today, I'll share more about what happened. It's a pretty wild story.

But previously to that, I was at another radio station. I did a talk show for twenty-one years, so I'm not unfamiliar to being behind a microphone and doing a program. Not the caliber of Frank's, as I sit here filling in. I was praying before I went on the air, thinking *I can't fill in for this guy*. His shoes are way too big. His persona is larger than life. But by the grace of God, I'm here in honor of Him and in relation to our Lord, who means everything to me.

So Happy Thanksgiving, a day we're supposed to give thanks. For so many years of my life, before I knew Jesus Christ, I thought Thanksgiving was a time when I ate good food, I sat around the table with some family members I loved and . . . some family members that I tried best to like.

And that's how I began the three hours, trying to replace a wonderful Christian man who happened to be a tremendous talk show host.

After the holidays, Chuck asked me if I would become one of a handful of guest hosts filling in for Frank. I said yes without hesitation.

The lid on information about Frank's condition was kept on tight. I really didn't know exactly how Frank was doing, but as one week stretched into two, it was apparent that Frank was in a fight for his life. I desperately wanted to visit him in the hospital. I knew the family couldn't say yes to everyone, but I was relieved when I received the okay to see him after speaking with his wife, Gina. She reiterated that everything was hush-hush.

When I approached the nurses' station at the USC Medical Center that afternoon, an RN asked me, "Are you Frank's brother?" She wasn't the first to say that we looked alike, from our body builds and olive complexion to the shiny domes atop our heads. I smiled and said I wasn't his brother, but I appreciated the sentiment.

I walked into the private room and saw Frank lying in a hospital bed, hooked up to all sorts of tubes and beeping monitor devices. He had a breathing apparatus through his throat; it was clear he wasn't breathing on his own. Casts were wrapped around both legs and one arm. His face was unblemished, but I had trouble immediately recognizing him. He was visibly thinner than the last time I had seen him in October.

"If you're going to talk to him, you should yell at him," Gina said.

I didn't have it in my heart to raise my voice to Frank. Instead, I leaned close and whispered to him. I told him how much I loved him and how much he meant to Erin and me. Then I thought he'd appreciate a moment of levity.

"Just hang in there," I said. "They're letting me fill in for you on the air, which just goes to show you that they'll let just about anyone do your show, so you better come back. So you get well soon. I love you . . ."

Frank was totally unresponsive.

I left the medical facility sobered by the experience. It did not look good.

I generally filled in for Frank around once a week through early December. As days turned into weeks and Frank remained in a coma, I steeled myself to receive the news that his physical body was no longer alive but that he was alive with Christ in heaven.

Twenty-eight days after he went down on the 210, and twenty-eight years after my motorcycle accident, Frank Pastore died on December 17, 2012—exactly three years to the day after I gave my life to Christ in a parking lot adjoining the Fullerton Municipal Golf Course.

As I've been telling people ever since, you can't make this stuff up.

23

BREAK ON THROUGH

When Frank Pastore died, KKLA Vice President/General Manager Terry Fahy issued a statement: "On Monday, December 17, our beloved friend and co-worker, Frank Pastore, was ushered into the presence of Jesus. Although this was no surprise to the Lord, it hit Frank's wife, Gina, and their immediate family, and the KKLA family, extremely hard."

Me, too. I reeled from the loss. In many ways, from our similar Italian-American ancestry, Catholic upbringing, ages, similar looks, and coming-to-Christ-later-in-life stories, Frank felt like the brother I never had.

The question front and center in my mind was this: Who would succeed Frank as KKLA's afternoon drive-time host?

I knew the KKLA management was looking at several different people, including me. I had made Chuck Tyler and Terry Fahy aware of my great desire to succeed Frank.

Nothing was going to be decided over the Christmas holidays, not while everyone was still grieving. As the KKLA management deliberated during the first few months of 2013, I continued to guest host here and there.

I knew a big question mark hung over me. I figured the KKLA executives were thinking along these lines:

Frank has been a Christian for just three years. Our only live show each afternoon flies the KKLA flag and is an important forum for the issues of the day as well as pertinent topics on the hearts of our listening audience. The host must be able to stand on his (or her) own two feet on firm theological ground and be a witness for Christ as well as the values of this station.

KKLA executives painstakingly and prayerfully took their time. Talk about a faith-building exercise for me. And then I heard the great news in May—*Frank, you've got the job.*

I was officially announced as the new afternoon-drive talk host for KKLA on June 12, 2013. "I am both honored and humbled," I said in the official press release to the media. "This is a new season for KKLA and for me, and it is my hope that together we can make a difference in our community as we proclaim His Love and truth."

I knew I needed prayer—and needed to pray—to take on this responsibility. During the first month on the air, there were times when I'd be in the middle of voicing a thought or asking a question to a high-profile guest and I'd hear a loud voice in my head saying, *Who are you kidding? Who are you to sit in that chair?*

I knew it was the Deceiver. I would rebuke him in the name of Christ and by His authority.

Those were difficult moments. It was easier when my colleagues in the KKLA hallways joked that we didn't have to change the name of the weekly management meeting—called a "Frank Discussion"—held every Wednesday. Nor did the webmaster have much trouble fixing the KKLA website. All he had to do was insert "Sontag" for "Pastore" in the show name and find another head shot of a bald guy.

The studio from where I did the show was the same place where Frank interviewed me in 2012. Fittingly, that studio was renamed "Frank Pastore Studio B" in his honor.

I continued to be completely trusting in the Lord to lead me. I brought on captivating guests. Presided over interesting discussions. Engaged callers. And embraced the challenge of live Christian radio.

As I gained my sea legs in the first few months on the air, I believed I really was one of the most blessed people on this earth to host the *Frank Sontag Show* on KKLA.

ONE YEAR LATER

As we neared the one-year anniversary of Frank's death on December 17, 2013, I knew we needed to do a tribute show marking Frank's passing. In my mind, that meant having one person join me in the studio: Gina Pastore.

Gina was courageous to come on the air and carry on Frank's legacy. "In fact, you and I have been talking about not crying today," she said early in the show. "We are doing pretty good so far. Yeah, Frank had a very sensitive side. He cried a lot. We would go to the movies, and I would look over and he would be sobbing. And I would sort of tear up and I would think, *Why is he crying so much?*

"This past year, I will tell you that I cried more than he ever did. He was a man's man, but he loved women and I mean that in a respectful way. He respected me tremendously and he loved the women that he worked with. He was a man's man, but he was also a gal's man."

Gina and I spent two hours reminiscing about Frank and conducting live interviews over the phone with a series of Christian notables, like Jim Daly, president of Focus on the Family, Dr. James Dobson, the founder of Focus on the Family and host of *Family Talk*, and former Athletes in Action president Wendell Deyo.

As we brought the emotional show to a close, I looked Gina in the eyes. "Gina, Erin and I love you a great deal, and after sitting in this chair and talking about your husband, I can only say that I know exactly what our guests were talking about today. I loved Frank a lot. He set the bar so high for doing this program, and I aspire to that every day. I pray that some day I'll look at him, and he'll laugh at me say, 'Well, bro, how was it? Not as easy as you thought, right?'"

You're right, Frank. Following you isn't easy.

But I never expected an easy ride.

EPILOGUE

On March 31, 2014, as I was finishing *Light the Way Home*, my step-mom called with unexpected but inevitable news: my father had passed away. He was eighty-one years old.

Following Dad's retirement from the movie industry in 2005, he and Anita moved to Homedale, Idaho, around forty miles west of Boise. They enjoyed eight golden years together until his sudden death. The last time I spoke to him was around ten days earlier.

As our discussion came to an end, I said, "Take it easy, Dad. I love you and miss seeing you. Erin and I will come up with Dante in June."

"I love you, too," Dad said, which felt great to hear. We had reconciled twenty years earlier through the *Mark & Brian Show*, of all things. On the Friday before Father's Day in 1993, Mark and Brian urged listeners to clean things up with their fathers, to make things right. If listeners needed help, then Mark and Brian would help facilitate the healing process—on the air, of course.

That day, I blurted, "I haven't talked to my dad in three years." There was a reason for that. Dad and I were estranged. We weren't on speaking terms because of my disappointment with him over the years and how he wasn't there for me.

Mark and Brian called my father, who picked up his phone. They explained the situation to my father—about making things right—and then invited me to join in. "Dad," I said, "I'm sorry I haven't called in all these years. I want to make things right with you because you're my dad and I love you."

Once I expressed my love for my father, I could feel the walls tumbling down.

"That's wonderful to hear, son. I love you, too."

Dad was nothing but sweetness and light the entire time we talked on the air. This wasn't a feel-good stunt on anyone's part—it worked. From then on, Dad and I spent quality time with each other. We both felt reconciled.

Flash forward more than twenty years and Anita's phone call informing me that my father had peacefully died that morning at home, in his bed. His breathing got labored, and then he stopped breathing. There was no pain at the end.

The last time I saw him was during Thanksgiving in 2013, after I had been named as the new host of the *Frank Sontag Show* on KKLA. Erin, Dante, and I drove to Idaho to spend nearly a week with him and Anita. He knew of my conversion experience, of course, and he thought it was great that I was working for the preeminent Christian radio station in Southern California. He told me several times how proud he was of me. That made me feel good. Really good.

Before we left to return to California, I said, "Dad, I really want to share with you that I want to see you in heaven some day. I really want you to know Jesus Christ."

"I know Him," he said, tugging at the Catholic cross around his neck.

Dad didn't want to say much more. He came of age at a time when people were told that "religion" was a private matter and not discussed in public. Having a personal relationship with Christ wasn't emphasized in the Catholic Church. Duty and following rules were.

The last time we spoke on the phone, Dad did something out of character for him. We usually ended our conversations with him saying, "No stunts." That was his way of saying, *Be careful out there, son.*

On this occasion, Dad didn't say, "No stunts."

To me, this moment in time was like the passing of the baton, a figurative reversal of roles. I sensed that *I* was supposed to tell him that.

"No stunts, Dad," I said. *Be careful. You're nearing that Day.*

"Okay, son."

I told this story on the day after his death on the *Frank Sontag Show.* Before my father's passing, I had scheduled Philip De Courcy, senior pastor of Kindred Community Church in Anaheim Hills. I kept the appointment, and I was glad we did. For nearly ninety minutes, we shared a fascinating conversation on the air. Philip spoke at great length about the "ministry of death," as he called it.

During the show's final segment before the six o'clock hour, I had the microphone to myself. I finished the show with this:

> We've been talking life and death and grief and fear and hope, and I want to speak to you right now.
>
> My father passed away yesterday. A man that in my younger days I admired a great deal, even though we actually had a horrible, horrible relationship for many years, if I can be honest here. Praise God, in the ensuing years, we reconciled and made amends. In the last couple of decades of my dad's life, we left nothing unsaid.
>
> Have you left something unsaid? Part of the reason I wanted to do the broadcast today is to appeal to you that if you don't know Jesus Christ, if you don't know Him, and would like to accept Him, you can do that now. Maybe you'd like to recommit your life to Christ.
>
> So do you know Jesus Christ? If you don't, I invite you to pray the Sinner's Prayer with me right now. If you feel ready to surrender and follow Jesus Christ, then say the following words:
>
> *Dear Lord Jesus, I know that I'm a sinner, and I ask for your forgiveness. I believe You died for my sins and rose from the dead. I turn from my sins right now and invite you to come into my heart and life. I want to trust and follow You as my Lord and Savior from this moment on. In Jesus name, I say amen.*

This was not the first time I invited KKLA listeners to repent of their sins and ask Jesus Christ to come into their hearts so that they could have eternal life with Him.

And it won't be the last time I light the way home.

ABOUT THE AUTHORS

Frank Sontag, the host of the *Frank Sontag Show* heard six times a week on KKLA 99.5 FM in the Los Angeles area, took an unlikely route into radio. Following high school graduation, he worked ten years in the grocery business for supermarket chains such as Ralph's and Gelson's. He then moved into radio in 1987 as the host of *Impact*, a talk show on spirituality that aired Sunday nights on KLOS 95.5 FM in Southern California.

He also became the engineer of the highly successful *Mark & Brian Show* on KLOS, heard weekday mornings. A late-in-life conversion experience as well as the end of the *Mark & Brian Show* in 2012, after twenty-five years on the air, led him to KKLA, where he succeeded the late Frank Pastore as the afternoon drive-time talk show host. He has been hosting the *Frank Sontag Show* since the summer of 2013.

Frank and his lovely wife, Erin, are the parents of Dante and live in Porter Ranch, California.

His website is www.franksontag.net.

Mike Yorkey, a veteran writer, is the author or co-author of more than eighty-five books with more than 2 million copies in print. He has collaborated with Tampa Bay Rays' Ben Zobrist and his wife, Julianna, a Christian music artist, in *Double Play*; Cleveland Browns quarterback Colt McCoy and his father, Brad, in *Growing Up Colt*; San Francisco Giants pitcher Dave Dravecky in *Called Up*; San Diego Chargers placekicker Rolf Benirschke in *Alive & Kicking*; tennis star Michael Chang in *Holding Serve*; and paralyzed Rutgers' defensive tackle Eric LeGrand in *Believe: My Faith and the Tackle That Changed My Life*. Mike is also the co-author of the internationally bestselling *Every Man's Battle* series with Steve Arterburn and Fred Stoker.

He and his wife, Nicole, are the parents of two adult children and make their home in Encinitas, California.

Mike's website is www.mikeyorkey.com.

INVITE FRANK SONTAG TO
SPEAK AT YOUR CHURCH
OR COMMUNITY EVENT

Frank Sontag is a gifted communicator who loves teaching others how to let Jesus Christ light the way in your life. He's also a dynamic and emotional speaker with a passion to share a countercultural message that all paths do not lead to God. Frank is available to speak in church pulpits, men's and women's weekend conferences, and vacation retreats.

If you, your church, or your community organization would like Frank to come speak at your event, contact:

Phil Van Horn
Integrity Sports Agency LLC
301 N. Lake Ave, 7th Floor
Pasadena, CA 91101
(818) 517-5880 cell
BallPhild@gmail.com

For bulk purchases of *Light the Way Home*, please contact Phil Van Horn.